Hope Heals

A Story about Faith, Hope, and Healing

DIANE GRUBER-STRICKLAND

PROFESSIONAL PUBLISHING MEETS POWERFUL PROMOTION

A wholly owned subsidiary of TBN

A Wholly Owned Subsidiary of Trinity Broadcasting Network

2442 Michelle Drive

Tustin, CA 92780

Copyright © 2021 by Diane Gruber-Strickland

All Scripture quotations, unless otherwise noted, taken from THE HOLY BIBLE, NEW INTERNATIONAL VERSION®, NIV® Copyright © 1973, 1978, 1984, 2011 by Biblica, Inc.® Used by permission. All rights reserved worldwide.

All rights reserved, including the right to reproduce this book or portions thereof in any form whatsoever.

For information, address Trilogy Christian Publishing

Rights Department, 2442 Michelle Drive, Tustin, Ca 92780.

Trilogy Christian Publishing/ TBN and colophon are trademarks of Trinity Broadcasting Network.

For information about special discounts for bulk purchases, please contact Trilogy Christian Publishing.

Manufactured in the United States of America

Trilogy Disclaimer: The views and content expressed in this book are those of the author and may not necessarily reflect the views and doctrine of Trilogy Christian Publishing or the Trinity Broadcasting Network.

10 9 8 7 6 5 4 3 2 1

Library of Congress Cataloging-in-Publication Data is available.

ISBN 978-1-63769-406-0

ISBN978-1-63769-407-7 (ebook)

Dedication

This book was written in honor of the three most remarkable and influential people in my life: my mom, Betty Jane Gruber, my beautiful daughter, Kristin, and my wonderful, loving husband, Steve.

My mother was always known as a woman of incredible strength, unfaltering faith, and an incredible love for her family, friends, and neighbors. Whenever someone she cared about was sick, injured, or experiencing the loss of a loved one, she was always the first one to make and deliver a meal to them, and always with a huge smile.

As a farm wife she was constantly busy doing something, whether it was tending to her large vegetable garden, canning or freezing, cooking or baking for her large family, helping dad in the fields, or milking the cows. But first and foremost, her biggest love was being a mother to her eight children.

It was her dedication as a mother, her strong faith, and her continual support that encouraged me to seek out my God-given purpose and the determination to see it through to the end. She has always been my biggest fan.

My daughter, Kristin, with her kind heart and easy-going nature, has always been quick to encourage me forward and was the driving force behind most of my accomplishments. Navigating life through the early part of her years within a single-parent household, she learned at a very young age to be strong and independent. She also grew up with the realization that she could accomplish anything she wanted, if she believed in herself and worked hard enough at it. Although we had our challenges along the way, in the end she was and is my truest and best friend.

To my devoted and loving husband, Steve, my best friend and partner. There is no one on earth I'd rather be going through life with. Although a bit skeptical at first of my new endeavor, he eventually warmed up to it once he saw how determined and dedicated I was to seeing it through. And after witnessing the amazing connection between horse and child and the positive effects of the ministry, he became our biggest support system, our backbone, the glue and strength that held us together. No matter how busy life gets for him, he is always there whenever we need him—whether it's a request to fix something in the barn, to lend a helping hand, or to give advice and share his invaluable wisdom.

These three very important people in my life, although not always seen, became the most significant force working behind the scenes of this important ministry called Hope's Haven.

Acknowledgements

Hope Heals was written in honor of all the spectacular volunteers at Hope's Haven, past and present, who work tirelessly each and every day, doing their part to ensure that the horses are cared for and that everything runs smoothly. Whether it be mucking stalls, assisting the farrier or vet, pulling weeds, fixing fences, working horses, or mentoring the youth who walk through our doors, our volunteers always come together like family, rubbing elbows and sharing dirt to get the job done. Just as our motto describes: "Many hands; one heart; one vision."

The acknowledgements listed below were written specifically for our current dedicated volunteers, as well as those who have shouldered with us for a year or more.

Brenda S, our barn manager and horse care coordinator; with her feisty, bubbly personality and fun-loving schemes, she always makes our time at the barn exciting and adventurous. She can be a "tuff" gal at times, but she always gets the job done. And with her big heart, she always goes above and beyond to do for others.

Vicki, our lesson instructor and session leader, who leads the way with her smart, witty charm and firm demeanor. Her creativeness and big heart are a true blessing to our mentorship program. She has a soul for music and a love for kids. She has helped to create a strong, faith-centered foundation in which to serve our troubled youth. Along with her two young'uns, Felicity and Phineas, she sets a prime example of what it means to work hard toward a common goal.

Margaret, our solid-as-a-rock support person. Her sweet, caring, hardworking, dependable self makes it so easy to love her. When it comes to working around the kids and horses, she is always happy and eager to lend a hand. A valuable addition to our mentorship program, she is a true gift. And for a special bonus, Margaret regularly blesses us with her delicious home-baked goodies.

Laurie, our strong, wise, and fearless mentor. With years of experience and knowledge in running a non-profit and working with troubled youth, Laurie has become a very valuable addition to our Hope's Haven family. She has become our trailblazer, forging our path forward to a bigger, stronger future. With her administrative skills, she has graciously created templates for our newsletters, fundraising flyers, and labels, as well as supplying many other needs.

Carson: With his genuine interest in exotic animals and in becoming a veterinarian, he is always ready to lend a hand and help out where needed, especially when any of our horses are in need of any type of first aid treatment.

Donna B, our warrior and crusader, fighting against all the injustice and animal cruelty in the world. If a horse or other animal needs saved anywhere, Donna is on it! She is a very strong, industrious individual who doesn't know the meaning of laziness or giving up. If there's ever a job that needs done, she will get 'er done. Another valuable addition to our mentorship program, she definitely has a soft spot for the kids, and it shows. From marketing to fundraising to needed construction projects, Donna blazes on...

Pam, our quiet, tender-hearted saint. The first to offer a helping hand, and the last to ever complain. She's a whiz with the kids and crafty as can be; her patience and creativity are sure a pleasantry. Always so dependable, she is someone we can always count on, no matter what.

Alyssa, one of our initial junior volunteers, who was with us from the beginning. She walked through our doors into the mentorship program timid and unsure, only to emerge as a confident young lady two years later. Her charm won our hearts, and her patience and compassion made her a winner with the kids. She may have appeared "lost" when she came to us, but after she found her equine friend

Zeke, together they helped each other grow and heal.

April T, our serious, "get the job done" persona. With her great work ethic and dependability, she always showed up rain or shine to do her part in barn work, horse care, and assisting at fundraisers. Her only fault was her consistent footwear fashion statement. One of our barn rules is "must wear close-toed shoes at all times when in the barn or working around the horses." I can't tell you how often she was spotted wearing her infamous flip-flops.

Amanda, inquisitive and funny. Though she initially arrived at Hope's Haven with little horse knowledge or experience, I've witnessed her growth as she's navigated the course to learning all about horse care, barn work, and being a session leader.

Laura, sweet and dependable. Always willing to fill in and help out as needed. She initially came to Hope's Haven at our fall fundraiser, Hope's Hoedown. It was here that she met her heart horse, Mikey, and weeks later officially adopted him. She plays an important role on our horse care wellness team, ensuring all horses are well fed and cared for.

Sue, one of our "newbies" and a recently retired school teacher, offers such a sweet soul and kind spirit. A health and fitness guru, she ensures that the kids and volunteers stay fit. New to horses and barn work, she has worked hard to learn the ropes and is a wonderful addition to our mentorship program, and has become a wonderful session leader.

Krystle, our charismatic, fun-loving "newbie," has blazed the trail to becoming a stellar session leader and horse handler. Always willing to lend a hand and help out whenever needed.

Ronnie, our lawn keeper and weed whacker, is always willing to help keep the grounds looking well-manicured and clean. He loves grooming and taking care of the horses, especially his boy, Oats.

Rebecca T, our wise, kind, and big-hearted spiritual leader. Rebecca came to us from New Jersey with not an ounce of horse knowledge. But with a determined heart and a lot of genuine dedication, she quickly learned all there was to know about caring for horses, whether it was newly-rescued horses or our program horses. This sweet, I'll-do-anything-for-ya gal is the person you want on your team, and on your side, forever. Such a soft-spoken, hard worker, she also has a fierce side that will surface in an instant if she ever feels that a loved one is being hurt or threatened.

Rachel, a.k.a. Rebecca's daughter, appeared at Hope's Haven with her mom, shy, quiet, and unsure. Having dealt with personal trauma in her recent past, she appeared to be shut down and struggling to find her way in a cruel and uncertain world. After a few months of volunteering at Hope's Haven and spending time with the horses, especially a recent rescue named Belle, I witnessed this quiet, timid girl become a confident, strong, and happy young lady who would talk my ear off if given the chance. Her contribution to Hope's Haven includes caring for the rescued and retired horses, assisting with the website, and creating promo videos.

Donna K (a.k.a. Dee), our landscaping and gardening expert. Another DIY extraordinaire. Donna has a wealth of knowledge to contribute and is just as hardworking. In the short time she's been with us, she has gone to great lengths to make Hope's Haven more functional and beautiful. I don't know what we ever did without her. With a big heart for kids, she has become a valuable leader of our mentorship program.

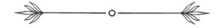

A very special thank you to our wonderful Junior Volunteers:

Kylie, Zoe, Abby, Serenah, and Brooke.

Never have I witnessed such growth and maturity as I have this past year with the junior volunteers. These kids have proven themselves beyond words. They have worked hard, learning the ropes of daily horse care, barn work, and working with the horses. I wholeheartedly trust each and every one of them just as much as I do the adult volunteers. Kids today could learn so much from each and every one of these extraordinary youth. I'm so proud of you and your accomplishments.

Introduction

As I walked through the dark, chilly barn lined with rows and rows of sickly, injured, and starving horses, I had no idea exactly what I was looking for. My past experiences have taught me that it's not myself who picks the horse—they, in fact, pick me. In an instant, they lock gazes as they look my way with empty but desperate eyes, pleading for me to notice them—to give them a second look, a gentle stroke of my hands, and a second chance at a new life—hoping it will be a life full of love, patience, and kindness, because the only life they have known up to this day has been one of abuse, neglect, or hunger.

As I rounded the corner and walked into the east wing of the auction barn, I saw her. She appeared tiny standing next to the taller horses. Her coat was dull and covered with multiple cuts and scrapes. I could see her ribs and hip bones sticking out as she moved about the tight quarters of her stall, where she would spend the next several hours. Then, as though it took great effort, she turned and looked at me. There was an emptiness in her eyes, and her only concern at the moment was the hay in front of her that she was hungrily munching on. She was obviously sick, beaten down, and broken, but somewhere deep beneath the darkness in her eyes, I saw a glimmer of hope—a sign that seemed to scream that not all was completely lost.

As quickly as she turned to look at me, she removed her gaze and returned to the task in front of her, but not before I was able to catch the pleading look in her eyes.

On the contrary, she barely noticed me standing there, nor my attempt to comfort her and draw her in. She was detaching herself from mankind in a desperate attempt to self-preserve. It was at this moment that I knew I had to step up and do something to save this ragged, beaten-down, broken horse.

And so, this is how the story began for this buckskin mare named Hope.

Table of Contents:

"My Broken Wings" is a heartfelt poem, written a long time ago, that tells the story of the strong bond formed between a young girl (myself) and her devoted, forever-loyal best friend—her horse, Apache.

My Broken Wings

With a heavy heart, I looked up and saw her watching me,
Knowing all my pain and sadness she could now see;
Hesitantly, I got up and slowly walked toward her,
Beginning to cry when she put her head on my shoulder.

Such a dependable friend, she was always there,
To show me in her quiet way that she really does care;
With a small whinny that means she's glad to see me,
Rubbing her velvety-soft nose against my cheek when she's happy.

But today was different, and she knew something was wrong,
So, she became my crutch, like a true friend to remain strong;
I gave her a hug and looked into her big brown eyes,
Knowing there wouldn't be enough time for good-byes.

Getting impatient, she gave me a small push with her head,
As if to say, "Let's just go, and forget those days ahead."
So, I climbed into the saddle, ready to take the last flight,
Trying not to think of the future as we headed into the night.

As she broke into a run, my troubled mind began to clear,
Caring only for the one beneath me who's always been so dear;
Girl and horse, we were then riding as one,
Going further into the night and having so much fun.

We rode by frost-covered fields and shallow streams,
Lit only by a harvest moon, so beautiful it now seems;
As she ran with her mane flowing, her feet going faster,
She gave me wings to fly, so now any problem I could master.

I soared through the air; my wings made me strong,
Given to me by my friend who could do no wrong;
But my wings soon broke the day that she had to leave,
I didn't want to let go; in my heart I tried to cleave.

I can still see her ears flicker when she hears my voice,
Oh, why did I have to go and make such a stupid choice?
I hear her whinny, and I know she's calling to me,
But her once-vivid face I can no longer clearly see.

I feel her head pushing me like she used to do,
As if she's telling me to stop feeling so blue;
But I drag myself through the day, hoping someday she'll again be mine,
Knowing deep down that one day, my dear friend I will find.

Yet still, I'm waiting, with a heart that no longer sings,
For she made me strong, but now all I have are my broken wings.

Chapter 1

Jax in the Box

Acts 16:24

"When he received these orders, he put them in the inner cell and fastened their feet in the stocks" (New International Version).

I've always been a firm believer that you should follow your heart and listen to your gut. I have found this to be especially true when it comes to rescuing horses. The old adage that "you don't pick the horse, the horse picks you" couldn't be truer. I distinctly remember how I came about finding my first rescue, Jax. I am not one who surfs the internet frequently, so when I had such a strong urge to check out a particular site, I immediately typed in the name and clicked go. As I scrolled through the list of horses featured on this site, one in particular caught my eye. He was a beautiful twelve-year-old sorrel and white paint gelding. While reading through the brief description and watching the riding video, this clumsy-looking paint tugged on my heartstrings. He was trying so hard to do what his rider was asking of him as he stumbled along, looking so exhausted and lost. As the deadline approached to bail the last of the horses, this beautiful paint was one of the few left standing. He looked so sad, his eyes pleading for someone to save him. I picked up the phone to make the call, hoping I wasn't too late. Once I paid bail for him, the lady on the other end of the phone told me, "Five minutes more and he would have been loaded onto the slaughter truck."

As soon as I got off the phone, I contacted someone to pick up my newly-rescued horse and transport him to a quarantine facility. The lady I chose, fortunately, was able to provide both the transport and quarantine. She told me that she'd pick him up in two days, which was on a Thursday. I was so elated and excited at the same time. There was no better feeling than this; knowing that my actions to step forward and save this horse—who otherwise would have been loaded onto the slaughter truck—made me feel like I had truly made a difference in this horse's life that night. I couldn't wait till the day came when I could go see him. That day finally came, four days after I had made the call that forever changed this horse's destiny. As I drove down the stone driveway that led to the barn, I could barely contain my excitement. I entered the barn and walked down the aisleway, looking for the sorrel and white paint that had stolen my heart. As I reached the last stall, I heard faint voices coming from outside the barn, so I made my way out and around to the back of the barn. The woman I had spoken to on the phone when I arranged his transport met me as I rounded the back corner of the barn and approached the outside stalls. As she led me to the paint's stall, I was suddenly taken aback by the pitiful sight that stood before me. This couldn't be the horse I had seen on the dealer's site just a few days ago. This horse appeared very ill and thin; the hollow, fearful look I saw in his eyes will be burned into my memory for the rest of my life. He was standing at the far end of his square concrete stall, totally detached from anything that was going on around him.

Jax, at the quarantine farm, shortly after being rescued

With his body turned away from us, he didn't even look my way when I offered him treats. My attempts to draw him in and make contact were futile as he completely ignored me and showed no interest whatsoever. Feeling defeated, I stepped back out of his stall, and taking a much closer look at him I noticed some very distinct markings. One was a half-moon shape on his forehead that appeared to look like a backwards letter J. Another marking was a large, oblong-shaped X on his left shoulder, and on his right shoulder, sitting in a sideways position, was the letter A. Looking at these "signs," it became very clear to me what his new name would be. From this day forward, he was called "Jax."

After spending some time with him and saying farewell to the nice lady, I headed back out to my car feeling rather deflated. This was not at all what I had thought it would be. I expected this new rescue horse to be all over me with gratitude, loving up this person who had saved him from a most certain and horrific death. Instead, I witnessed a scared, desolate animal, totally detached from the human world. Little did I know then what it would take to break through the four walls that this rescue horse had erected around himself. Like most horses who have lived through the peril of abuse and neglect, they disconnect in their final efforts to self-preserve whatever dignity and strength they have left. Ultimately, they let go of whatever love or attachment they once felt for a human being and retreat somewhere so deep, and so far down inside themselves—a place where the betrayal and rejection don't hurt them so much anymore.

At this phase of quiet desperation, one might notice the hollow emptiness in their eyes. The same eyes that once held a spark of hope and light that was now replaced with fear and hopelessness.

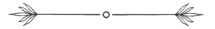

So, it was with Jax that this chapter in my life began. The chapter that ultimately led me through many tumultuous rescue adventures in the years to come.

Chapter 2

The Homecoming

Revelation 21:4

"He will wipe away every tear from their eyes, and death shall be no more, neither shall there be mourning, nor crying, nor pain anymore, for the former things have passed away" (English Standard Version).

When it was time for Jax to leave quarantine, I arranged for him to be transported to the stable where I was boarding my personal horse, Rita. As we anxiously awaited his arrival, I got his stall ready and made sure he had plenty of hay, water, and soft bedding.

I was pacing back and forth in the barn when I heard the truck approaching outside. Within minutes, Jax was unloaded and settled into his stall without issue. It was as if he knew he was truly safe now. Before I left him to head home, I gave him a big hug and assured him he would never have to endure an auction house, abuse, neglect, or hunger ever again.

Two weeks later it was time for Jax to be evaluated under saddle, so he could be successfully paired up with his new, forever adoptive family.

As trainer Jeff quietly led him out to the riding arena and prepared to lunge him, I stood quietly outside the fence, watching. I could tell that this was probably his first time ever being lunged, because he was all over the place, and it was quite obvious that he didn't know what to do or what the trainer was asking of him. After several more minutes of lunging, the trainer grabbed the saddle and gently laid it onto Jax's back. With no resistance seen, he proceeded to climb into the saddle for the riding eval. Suddenly, the most unexpected thing happened. It was as if an invisible switch suddenly flipped inside Jax's head, and what I witnessed next was the behavior of a very different horse. This seemingly quiet horse suddenly turned into a wild, bucking bronco. As he flew around the arena, kicking up a cloud of dust in a type of frenzied, erratic bucking, he quickly tossed the trainer off his back and onto the hard gravel. Jeff pulled himself up from the ground, brushed the dirt from his pants and exclaimed, "Well, I think it's quite obvious that this horse was never broke. So, it looks like we will hafta start from scratch with him." The next few sessions primarily consisted of lunging, communicating, and connecting with Jax.

A few weeks later Jeff announced that he would no longer be able to continue with Jax's training, so Jax and Rita were moved to another stable and a new trainer was assigned to Jax. Within two months, Belinda had Jax broke and was riding him every day. It was time to advertise him for adoption. Amazingly, the first family that came to see him absolutely fell in love with him and completed an adoption contract on the spot. They wanted to adopt Jax and give him as a Christmas gift to their youngest son, Austin. "He will be so surprised," his mother said. They then got in their car and left, after making plans to return in one month with their trailer to take Jax home.

Those four weeks flew by so quickly, and the day finally arrived for Jax to go to his new, forever home. "This moment came all too quickly," I quietly said to myself. From the moment I had first spotted him on the kill pen site, to experiencing his transformation from hopeless and rescued to hopeful and re-homed, it seemed so surreal. I took a long, deep breath, bracing myself for the inevitable.

Through a small cloud of dust, I watched as their truck pulled down the long stone driveway, towing the large trailer behind them. I felt my heart lurch out of my chest. I wasn't prepared for what I was feeling. These last four months I'd known Jax, I had become quite attached to him. Letting go of him now, even though I knew he would have a great home, was a lot harder than I had ever imagined.

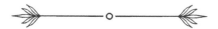

As Rita and Jax said their good-byes, I felt tears well up in my eyes and a sick feeling in the pit of my stomach. It wasn't supposed to be this hard. I felt myself drift off as my mind slowly wandered back to the day Jax had first arrived at the boarding stable. Rita had not been pleased by his arrival and did not welcome him at all. In fact, for days she put up quite a fuss with him, and not in a positive way. But Jax was quite the charmer, and it wasn't long before she warmed up to this handsome paint; shortly after arriving at Belinda's property, they were inseparable. I truly believe Rita knew that Jax was leaving, and that they would never see each other again, when I saw her reach her head toward him and gently touch his nose. Following Rita's obvious act of affection and final farewell to her friend, I reached over and

Rita and Jax saying good-bye

gave Jax a huge hug, and with tears streaming down my face, bid him farewell. Jax was then walked onto the trailer, and after everyone said their good-byes, his new family climbed into their truck and slowly drove out of the driveway and quietly out of our lives. Jax was on his way to his new home in Chincoteague, Virginia. He would be living on Chincoteague Island, and his new job would be helping with the annual pony roundups.

A part of me was excited for Jax and his new life as I watched them slowly disappear down the driveway and out of sight- leaving a cloud of dust behind them. I knew in my heart I would miss him greatly.

Chapter 3

Peppy Personality

1 Peter 5:10

"And the God of all grace, who called you to his eternal glory in Christ, after you have suffered a little while, will himself restore you and make you strong, firm and steadfast" (New International Version).

It was one of the hottest days of summer, and I was in total dismay at what I saw as I walked through the auction barn. Horses were tied so close together that they could barely move. Some had cuts or wounds from previous abuse or injury. Others were being picked on by larger, more aggressive horses. The fear and/or brokenness I saw in every one of their eyes was heartbreaking.

When I walked outside, I was even more horrified at what I saw: horses were lined up side by side and tied to metal railings outside a cattle barn, forced to stand on the hard, hot concrete for several hours without any source of food or water. Most of these horses were extremely thin and appeared very weak and lethargic. I had once heard that this area was typically reserved for the kill pen horses, or those that have been bought by kill buyers and are most likely being shipped to slaughter. From what I could determine, the majority of these horses were either Standardbreds or Saddlebreds, otherwise known as horses that once were Amish carriage horses.

As I walked toward the other end of the auction yard, a group of horses to my right caught my eye. There were five horses crammed into a small, square, concrete pen. No water or hay was available to them either. They were very stocky-looking and appeared to be of Morgan or Quarter Horse descent, and there were no visible signs of illness that I could see. It's a well-known fact that horses coming from auction houses are most often carrying some form of infectious disease and need to be quarantined for at least thirty days.

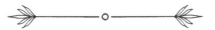

As I proceeded to walk past the concrete pen, one of the horses reached out through the railing and grabbed my shirt with his mouth, stopping me in my tracks. I turned to touch his face and saw a pleading look in his eyes. It was as if he was saying, "Wait! Look at me! Can't you *see* me?" I quickly glanced at the four horses in the pen with him. One had an injured leg and appeared crippled. The others jumped back and away from me when I attempted to touch them. This particular guy, however, was extremely friendly and social, if not a bit comical. Ironically, all five horses appeared to be of the same breed—maybe even related.

Peppy at the auction barn

As I was socializing with my newfound friend, a strange man walked by and scoffed, "Don't waste your time with this lot; they are all going on the slaughter truck as soon as the sale is over." Oh, no! I thought, *That's horrible! I cannot let that happen—not to this sweet boy.* So, with fierce determination, I set out on a mission: a mission to find out and locate the owner of this lot of horses. It didn't take long before I found someone who seemed to be familiar with the politics of this auction barn, so I decided to strike up a friendly conversation with her. Heather explained how she frequently visited auction barns and kill lots in an attempt to help horses in need. Within minutes, she had identified the kill buyer who owned the five horses and helped me locate him. He was a tall, stocky man with dark hair and a scruffy beard. He was as shrewd as he looked and made very clear the price that he wanted for each of the horses in the pen, and he would not back down. However, we were just as determined, and I was not leaving the barn without the sweet horse that had reached out and tugged on my heart.

Heather made her intentions very clear as well. She too planned to buy one of the other geldings in the lot. So, we fought even harder to make a deal with this man. "Two for one," we argued with him. "How do we even know if these horses can be ridden?" we asked. "Well," he said, "you can see for yourself in a minute; we are bringing them into the arena again as soon as the auction is over." Hearing this, we quickly turned away and headed back to the auction yard. We arrived just as a young girl was pulling "Mr. Personality" out of the pen and placing a bridle on him. She was rough as she handled him and showed no compassion in regard to his current dire situation. She quickly hopped onto his back and smacked him with the reigns, encouraging him forward. As he walked past me, he stopped and turned toward me, as if he was saying, "Please do something—help me!"

After watching the girl ride the two horses through the arena, we returned to the shrewd man, ready to make a deal. Heather had told me that it was likely that this man had not paid more than $500 per horse. Now, he was adamant in his asking price of $800 each.

I was feeling very angry as the blunt force of reality hit me: this man had most likely jacked the price up by $300 or more, only a couple of hours after he had initially purchased these horses. The realization surrounding this whole situation made me sick to the core, but also made me even more determined to win the game this cruel man was playing.

After what seemed like an eternity, and a very lengthy debate with this kill buyer, Heather and I walked away with two of the five horses, including the peppy, stocky horse that was full of personality.

Ironically, after the official transaction was completed and we were handed the sales slips and registration papers, we quickly glanced over the forms and realized that our initial instincts were correct all along. The five horses in that concrete pen were indeed related. In fact, the two we had fought so long and hard for were brothers.

"Mr. Personality's" registration paperwork listed his name as Peppy Pat Olena. So, that day marked a huge milestone in this stocky gelding's life, and he became known as Peppy personality.

Chapter 4
Hope's Purpose

Jeremiah 29:11

"'For I know the plans I have for you,' declares the Lord, 'plans to prosper you and not to harm you, plans to give you hope and a future'" (New International Version).

Hope's story of abuse and neglect ended that day at the auction house, and her second chance at a new life began. She was transported from the auction house to a beautiful farm in Maryland where she would spend the next sixty days in quarantine, getting healthy again. Little did she know that the day I spotted her at the sale barn, she was given a real purpose. She had been hand-picked to help a close friend through her journey to healing and recovery.

"Hope", shortly after arriving to our farm, after completing quarantine

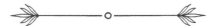

Lori, who would be turning thirty-eight years old, had recently been diagnosed with cervical cancer. A close friend and colleague

whom I worked with at a local hospital, she was fully aware of her prognosis. During the long and arduous road of chemo and radiation treatment, Lori found herself dealing with many emotional highs and lows and often in pain, sick, and absent from work. I remember on one occasion, while at work, Lori shared with me some of her recent struggles. As she spoke of her difficulties with treatment, I could sense her obvious disappointment in the lack of a strong support system. At a time when she needed him the most, her husband continued to fail her miserably. It was no secret that things were tense between the two of them, and that their marriage had been slowly spiraling downward for some time.

On this particular night, amidst the discussion of family affairs and cancer treatments, we found ourselves reminiscing over childhood memories and our love of horses. Lori was no stranger to my recent endeavors with rescuing horses, and we often spoke of their therapeutic benefits. After detailing the events surrounding the rescue of my most recent horses, Jax and Peppy, Lori revealed to me her life-long wish: she had always wanted a horse of her own, but circumstances had never allowed for it.

My friend had no idea that this particular conversation would set the wheels into motion for me to carry out the ultimate plan. Two weeks later, Hope was discovered at the auction house and rescued for a very special purpose. Now, it was time to carry out the plan and present Lori with her "gift."

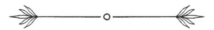

It was a cold, windy day in December, about a week before Christmas. I had plotted out how I would present this special gift to Lori. We met for breakfast at a local diner, then headed to the farm in Maryland where Hope awaited. Lori, being under the assumption that we were going to see another horse, Peppy, whom I had previously rescued from the kill pen, had no clue as to what was about to be unveiled.

We arrived at the farm and dove right into our normal ritual of feeding the horses carrot treats and spending lots of time with Peppy. As we were heading back to our vehicle, Lori glanced across the field to a smaller paddock, pointed at the buckskin quietly standing there looking at her, and exclaimed, "What's the story with that horse?"

"Well," I said, "let's go have a closer look at her. I believe she just arrived here a few days ago." As we approached the paddock that housed this beautiful but dilapidated mare, we noticed that she was cowering in the far corner, fearful of the other horses in the paddock. Hope was much smaller than the other two and was obviously being bullied by the larger horses. Even though she appeared fearful and unsure of the circumstances, she immediately came over to the side of the paddock where we stood. In an instant, we could see that she was very friendly, sweetly inquisitive, and craving attention. After only a few moments I could see a strong connection beginning to form between Hope and Lori, creating what was to be their next journey together.

Unfortunately, Hope was much sicker than we had first thought, and she needed to stay at the quarantine farm for another month. During this time, Lori and I planned regular trips to visit with her. It soon became a bi-weekly ritual, as we'd meet up at our favorite diner for breakfast, then begin our long trek to Thurmont, Maryland. During our visits, we looked forward to hearing updates on Hope's progress from the stable owner, Tim. Everyone seemed to agree that Hope definitely had a fighting spirit and a sweet, loving nature. "I'm surprised she's improving as quickly as she is; she really was a sick little horse," reported Tim. It was quite obvious that Hope was becoming a huge favorite at this busy but beautiful farm.

Chapter 5

A Not-So-Second Chance

2 Corinthians 5:17

"Therefore if any man be in Christ, he is a new creature: old things are passed away; behold, all things are become new" (**King James Version**).

After Peppy had finished sixty days of quarantine, he was moved to a beautiful stable in Thurmont, Maryland, until he could be moved home. While there, a trainer friend evaluated him and suggested he receive thirty to sixty days of training before he was adopted out. Two weeks later he left the beautiful stable and headed to her farm in Abbottstown, Pennsylvania, where he would learn how to be a horse again.

One month went by, and Belinda was giving me almost daily reports of Peppy's progress. He was learning slowly but willingly. "I don't believe he ever had any formal training before," Belinda said. "He acts like he doesn't understand what I'm asking of him." She went on to describe an incident that had happened the day before: "I was taking him through the paces in the arena, when suddenly he just turned and ran me into the wall. At this point I figured he was either purposefully trying to dump me, or he truly didn't know what I wanted from him. I will try working him every day for a while and see if that helps, but at this rate he's most likely going to need more than thirty days of training."

I tried to get there as often as I could to see him, but she lived over an hour away, and unfortunately it ended up being just two or three times a month. However, without fail, Peppy would be standing by the gate, ready to greet me whenever I came to visit. From what I saw he was such a lovebug, and he always wanted to be around people. He had this special way about him that always made my visits extra memorable. I remember one such time when I went to visit him at the farm in Maryland. When I arrived at his pasture, I couldn't locate him at first, so I called to him. Within seconds he appeared, running toward me from the farthest point of the pasture. He was the smallest horse in the field, but he didn't seem to care as he steamrolled through the cluster of tall horses that formed a wall between us; he just pushed right through them and came trotting over to me. I always had lots of carrot treats for him, and he would follow me everywhere. When my visit was over and I headed back to my car, he followed along with me on the other side of the fence, walking as far as the fence line would allow him to go. Then he just stood there, watching and waiting, as I drove down the long driveway and out of sight.

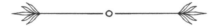

Forty-five days into his training, I received the most dreaded phone call from Belinda. Her voice seemed troubled as she struggled to find the right words. With a sharp breath, she proceeded to inform me that Peppy appeared to be favoring his left hind leg. She had noticed a limp that day during his training, and he had strongly resisted being ridden. "I think he's in pain, and that's why he was acting up," Belinda reported. "I'm gonna let him rest for a week and see if he improves." In the meantime, I agreed to have the vet examine him. So, we waited and prayed for his injury to heal, hoping it wasn't anything significant.

A week went by, and I had not heard any positive reports from Belinda. When she finally did call, it was not good news at all. The vet had been there that day, examined Peppy, and felt strongly that his injury was chronic and causing him a lot of pain. Unfortunately, he agreed with Belinda that the best course of action would be to euthanize him. Totally dumbfounded, I closed my eyes and took a long, ragged breath. How could this be? He seemed fine the last time I saw him. What could have possibly happened to have caused this so-called injury Belinda was talking about? Finding my voice, I explained that I would need to think about it. I had to have a few days to process this horrible news.

The next few days seemed endless and tortuous. How could I make this impossible decision? A decision which would ultimately decide his fate? Let him live, and hope and pray the injury was not chronic like the vet and trainer had reported? Or trust their expertise and knowledge to make the only compassionate choice there was, and finally end his pain and misery? The nightmares were endless, and I did not sleep well for days. That's when I knew—I had to go see Peppy. Seeing him would give me the answer and reassurance I needed to make this decision.

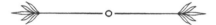

My legs didn't seem to want to move me forward as I climbed out of my car and began the trek down Belinda's driveway and up to the barn. As always, Peppy was standing at the gate, waiting for me. I gave him his usual carrot treats then stood quietly with him, just taking in the moment. Grabbing his lead from the nearby post, I clipped it onto his halter and opened the gate. As we walked toward the barn, I paid close attention to his gait and demeanor, specifically looking for any signs of pain or lameness. Besides appearing a bit jumpy and restless, I didn't see any obvious indications of injury. Once I got Peppy to the barn, I was able to assess him more closely. Belinda was nearby giving lessons and took a minute to point out where his injury was located below his left hind hock. Upon closer examination, I did see minor swelling and felt warmth at the site. At this time, Belinda informed me that he had also been acting aggressively since his injury, which she thought was most likely because of the pain he was experiencing. She went on to explain that during the last few weeks of training, he had either kicked at her, tried to bite her, run her into the arena wall, or attempted to unload her by dropping and rolling. On another occasion, he had busted through the gate and gotten out of the pasture.

Looking at my sweet Peppy now, I found her description of his behavior so hard to believe. I had never witnessed any aggressiveness from him, but most of my prior contact was before this proposed injury. We proceeded to walk Peppy to the small paddock behind the barn so he could get minimal exercise while allowing us to be able to fully assess him. I also wanted to give him the freedom to see the other horses, as Belinda was heading out on a trail ride with some students. It was during this time that I suddenly witnessed what Belinda had been describing to me.

Peppy appeared to be freaked out, running back and forth from one end of the paddock to the other. While observing all of this disorganized motion, I noticed a slight limp or hobbling as he bucked and ran about the paddock. When I attempted to talk to him and soothe him, he just ran past me, seemingly unaware of my presence as he almost plowed me over. I'll never forget the wild, frenzied, pained look in his eyes. This was a defining moment for me, and I knew then what my answer needed to be. Even though I had told Belinda I'd let her know my decision in a day or two, I knew in my heart what had to be done. After Peppy was safely returned to his pasture, I took a moment to discuss my concerns with Belinda. With the final decision behind me, I jumped into my car and pulled out of her driveway and away from the dark, stocky horse waiting at the gate. I believe that in his own way, he had just told me what I needed to do. I could not let him live with this frenzied pain. I loved him too much to continually see the torture in his beautiful eyes. The horse I saw at Belinda's that day was not the same teddy bear of a horse I had seen standing in the crowded kill pen just six months prior. As I drove farther away, I glimpsed in my rearview mirror for the last time the dark figure standing by the gate. It was as though he was saying good-bye. Rounding the corner and out of sight, I could barely see the road in front of me as tears were flowing down my face. The picture of him standing there, watching and waiting, will forever be burned into my memory. My Peppy personality, you not only grabbed at my shirt on that hot August day, but you also tugged on my heart and forever touched my soul. I will never forget you, my sweet, sweet boy.

Me and Peppy, at the quarantine farm in Maryland

Chapter 6

Hope's Healing

Matthew 4:23

Jesus Heals the Sick

"Jesus went throughout Galilee, teaching in their synagogues, proclaiming the good news of the kingdom, and healing every disease and sickness among the people" (New International Version).

As Lori journeyed through her chemo and radiation treatments, Hope was also continuing her journey to becoming well. As she finished the last few weeks of quarantine, she slowly began to put on some weight, and the spark returned to her eyes. Day by day we saw her true, playful personality returning. I often thought, *She must have really been loved by someone at one time, because she absolutely craves attention and to be loved on.* She was a real sweetheart, and a true diva.

It was more than sixty days from the start of her quarantine when Hope was cleared to come home. We were so excited as we arranged for her transport. As we drove to the quarantine farm to meet my friend who was transporting her, we discussed our plans for Hope once she arrived and got settled in her new home. Lori expressed her wishes to board Hope at Steve's and my farm, and her plans to visit often. She wanted to spend as much time with her as possible, so they could continue to create an even stronger bond.

Once Hope was loaded into the trailer we pulled in behind the truck, preparing to drive the two-hour trip to the farm. As we were driving along, taking in the beautiful countryside, I realized that we were beginning a whole new chapter in this story of rescuing horses and restoring hope—a chapter about pain, personal struggles, emotional battles, hope, healing, and triumph. Lori was fighting her own physical battle: a newly diagnosed form of aggressive cancer, its treatment, and side effects. But she was also dealing with personal struggles, as her marriage was continuing to dissipate.

Hope was dealing with her own struggles as well. Physically, she faced a long road of recovery from a severe respiratory illness. Plus, being very underweight, she was in need of lots of good nutrition. Often, I have found that horses in this type of situation are also very distrustful of humans. With Hope, however, that didn't seem to be the case. With her friendly, sweet, without-a-care-in-the-world persona, I was convinced that she must have really been valued and well cared for at one time. It made me wonder, *Is there someone out there who is missing Hope? Wanting her back, or even wondering where she is and what has happened to her?* I knew that if I had once owned a horse like Hope and for some reason had lost track of her, I would not quit until I found her again and knew she was okay.

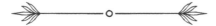

The arrival of spring brought with it the anticipation of new life and the explosion of many vibrant colors—blooming flowers, green grass, and budding trees. The world around us was coming to life in multi-dimensional beauty and the ever-so-sweet sensations of nature. With the emergence of this renewed life also came the restoration of spirit and increased strength. As Lori completed her final rounds of chemo and radiation treatments, the prognosis was looking very good for a full recovery and remission.

At the same time, Hope had fully recovered from her illness and was blossoming into a strong, healthy, beautiful horse. And as promised, Lori visited Hope often, thoroughly enjoying their time together while grooming and riding her around the farm.

Unfortunately, with the changing of the seasons often comes un-welcome changes in our lives, and although Lori had overcome her battle with cancer, she was now facing the dissolution of her mar-riage. With the summer's heat upon us and a marriage continuing to spiral downward, Lori made the difficult decision to surrender Hope back to me. This may have been the closing of a chapter in Lori's life, but it was the beginning of Hope's story, as she became the namesake for Hope's Haven Rescue and Youth Camp.

Hope and Lori, at me and Steve's farm

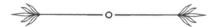

Little did I realize it at the time, but the final chapter in Hope and Lori's story opened up a whole new and exciting journey for Hope, and for everyone who entered the doors of Hope's Haven. The miraculous and awe-inspiring events we witnessed in the years to come couldn't have been anything short of God's own hand.

One such story began like any other normal day. We had a scheduled "meet n' greet" with a new family, a young boy and his grandmother. After the formalities were given, I led them down the aisleway of the barn and proceeded with my usual introductions of the horses, as I relayed each of their unique backstories. We didn't get any further than the first horse, Rita, when after I described her story of trauma and abuse, the young boy blurted out, "Well, I have a backstory too." Instantly, it was as though the flood gates burst open, and years of turmoil and pain gushed out. As this small, hurting boy told of his abuse and feelings of rejection and pain, Rita lowered her head, taking it all in, lending her ear and quiet acceptance.

This touching moment did not end with Rita, however. As the boy traveled down the aisleway, he quickly walked past the other horses and abruptly stopped at the "golden" horse's stall. I saw Hope reach out to him with her head, as she nuzzled him on the cheek as if giving him a kiss. There appeared to be a moment when time just stood still as I watched the silent communication transpire between this hurting boy and the horse. I knew instantly that something very special was taking place.

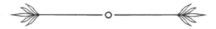

It was sometime later, after I had finished explaining our typical ninety-minute session routine—consisting of a thirty-minute chore, fifteen minutes of grooming, and ending with a designated activity with "your special horse"—that I walked outside to complete a task after asking the young boy to pick "his horse." It was at this particular moment, while outside, that I heard Hope kicking quite loudly against her stall door. *Oh no!* I frantically thought to myself, *Why, Hope, did you have to choose this specific moment to be a diva, vying for attention?*

Slowly, I walked back into the barn, certain that this boy would choose another horse because of Hope's little "temper tantrum" display. Hesitantly, I asked him if he had picked his special horse and was blown away when I heard his reply: "Yes, I want *Hope*!" With wide-eyed disbelief, I inquired, "Why? What exactly made you pick her?" It was then, to my complete amazement, that I heard the solemn conviction in his young voice when he replied, "Because she is attention-seeking, just *like me*."

Hope bonding with her new friend

Stories like this one, as I was soon to realize, were going to be a regular happening at Hope's Haven. As the mentorship season continued, we were able to witness God's hand in healing multiple times through His work with these special rescue horses. As mentors, we are given the unique opportunity to be special ambassadors for Him, guiding and encouraging young hearts forward to a place where they feel accepted and where hope is restored, allowing their bruised hearts to begin to heal. This is the great ministry He has called us to.

The young boy in this story went on to form a very unique bond with Hope that lasted all of two years. During this time, I got to witness a timid, scared, and hurting soul transform into a confident, talkative, and fun-loving young man, all because a "golden horse" reached out and touched his wounded heart.

Chapter 7

Honoring the Fallen

1 Thessalonians 5:13

"Hold them in the highest regard in love because of their work. Live in peace with each other" (New International Version).

The unspoken reality of the cruel and harsh practices that are often witnessed at sale barns and auction houses would leave you shaken to the core. To even try to conceive of such inhumane cruelty is difficult for anyone to imagine. Yet it still happens every day at auction barns across the United States. These innocent and helpless animals are completely defenseless against these brutal attacks, and they silently plead for someone to help them, to be their voice.

This is where animal rescue organizations play a huge part in assisting the helpless. Where caring people can really make a difference by standing up for what is right and changing the destiny of these precious animals.

The following heart-breaking story is true, and it happened at a local auction house just a few years ago. This story was taken from a local newspaper and the case was investigated, but no one was charged. The case went cold, and the horse was soon forgotten.

Sadly, this kind of treatment happens more often than we realize.

"Did Animal Cruelty Cause Horse's Death at Auction?"

"Pennsylvania authorities are currently investigating the death of a horse at a local horse auction barn. Individuals described as 'kill buyers' allegedly kicked the downed horse's weak and broken body prior to the animal's death Monday.

"A young girl who happened to be on the premises at the time commented that the alert, sweet, grey mare had caught her attention the previous day. She was at the horse auction videoing horses when she stopped and petted the big-eyed mare while looking her over. She had considered saving this sweet mare and wondered how she would feed this little mare if she were to come home with her.

"Unable to attend the auction on Monday, she however felt confident that another rescue would save the mare. Having been to this particular auction many times before, she knew for a fact that there would be many other equine rescues actively bidding on horses and particularly seeking out the weak, injured, and sickly 'high risk' horses.

"Unfortunately, as fate would have it, when she and a friend returned late Monday evening to pick up a horse from the auction for quarantine, she noticed a commotion on a nearby loading dock. As she and her friend got closer, they noticed a grey horse on the ground.

"It was at this time that they witnessed three men, reportedly kill buyers, prodding and kicking the horse, but the animal was unable to get up. The horse was still alive; they saw the mare moving her legs.

"Springing into action, she quickly offered to take the horse, but was told by one of the men, 'She's good as dead anyway.' It was at this moment that she realized it was the same grey mare she had contemplated saving the day before.

"The women witnessed the kill buyers loading another horse and a Belgian Draught horse, which 'stomped over the little grey mare who was down.'

"'When we got to her, she was still very much alive,' the woman added. The mare was trembling uncontrollably and gasping for breath.

"The young girl spoke gently as she softly caressed the mare's sweaty, lathered coat. 'I felt her heartbeat under my hand.' Before the frail, injured horse gasped her last breath, her eyes softened. Both girls were with her when she died.

"It was observed that the men left the auction property with their loaded livestock trailer full of horses before the grey mare died. The horse's body remained on the loading dock the entire night."

Understandably, the whole experience left her feeling utterly crushed, heartbroken., and extremely angry—angry at a world that is so heartless and cruel, to put such little value on one of God's most beautiful creations and to treat it so horribly.

*Story update: To our knowledge, nothing came of any "investigation" into this mare's death.

The preceding story contained the words that rippled across the headlines of a local newspaper back in mid- January, 2017.

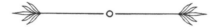

I knew all too well about the shady dealings that took place at this so-called auction house. I had frequented this sale barn many times, buying quite a few "slaughter bound" horses from the kill buyers, and was well aware of their reputation. As a matter of fact, I had personally met the young girl mentioned in the above article and had formed a sort of camaraderie with her.

After reading about this horrific tragedy, I contacted her, wanting to do something to remember and honor this fallen mare who had died so tragically. We both agreed wholeheartedly that we did not want her suffering to have been in vain. So, we talked for what seemed like forever and came up with a perfect plan. In two weeks we would meet at this auction barn and pick a horse that resembled the grey mare, and like her, was in need and at risk for slaughter. We would then purchase this horse from the kill buyer. Keirstin agreed to transport the horse to her rescue facility for quarantine and rehab. Then, when the horse was 100 percent well again, we would work together to get it adopted out to a forever home. Sounds like a good plan, right? Well, as all plans go, things don't always work out the way we hope.

When the day came for us to put this ingenious plan into action, Keirstin called me early that morning to inform me that she now had to work and couldn't meet me there. Extremely disappointed, but still determined to pull this off, we agreed I would still go to the auction barn. I would take pictures to send to her, and we would be in constant phone contact during the sale. This way, she would still be as involved in the task as possible.

I arrived at the auction house by 9:30 a.m. and entered the barn, figuring I'd make my way through the entire facility, checking out every horse, searching for a horse that looked like the grey mare. What I hadn't figured on was stumbling across a horse that chose me instead. As I made my way down a long aisle on the west side of the barn, I noticed a group of scraggly-looking, emaciated horses tied close together. Their appearance, however pathetic, somehow seemed hopeful. The whole group presented to be very friendly and calm. A few were dirty and covered with burrs so entangled in their manes and tails that it was difficult to make out their natural color. There was one that caught my eye immediately. He was a stout sorrel gelding with a wide blaze and one white sock on his left hind leg. As if on cue, he would turn and look directly at me every time I walked by. It was as if he was trying to get my attention, to get me to notice him.

Suddenly, as I was walking down the aisle, out of nowhere came a horse and rider barreling toward me. Without thinking, I jumped out of the aisle, landing beside the sorrel gelding. He never moved a muscle and didn't seem bothered at all by my abrupt appearance, or the disruption. As I moved closer to him, he wrapped his neck around me as if giving me a protective hug.

Chapter 8

A Horse Named Chief

Deuteronomy 31:6

"Be strong and courageous. Do not be afraid or terrified because of them, for the Lord your God goes with you; He will never leave you nor forsake you" (**New International Version**).

It was some time after our unexpected moment of bonding that I left the gelding and headed back to the auction arena. I wanted to be present when that specific group of horses came through, and I especially wanted to see who purchased the gelding. To my dismay, they never came through the auction. As soon as the sale ended, I jumped up and almost ran back to the west wing where the horses were stabled, but they were not there. *Where could they have gone?* I wondered. It seemed only a few minutes ago that I was standing there with the sorrel gelding. On a whim, I decided to walk over to the east wing and check out the dreaded area where most horses are held before being loaded onto slaughter-bound trucks. As I rounded the corner and glanced down the long row of horses tied by the loading docks, something familiar caught my eye. The sorrel gelding was looking my way, his head held high above the mountain of other horses. It was as if he was shouting, "Hey, here I am! I'm still here, but not for much longer." I suddenly realized that I needed to do something, and do it fast! As I glanced around, looking for reinforcements, my eyes fell on the face of a fellow rescue person who ironically had helped me with a former rescue just five months earlier. Within minutes, she discovered which dealer currently owned this gelding and helped me track him down. What followed next was two hours of grueling, heated debates between myself, Heather, and the dealer. To make matters worse, it was late January, with bitter cold temps, and it was snowing heavily outside and piling up fast.

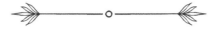

In the meantime, I received a phone call from Keirstin. She had a friend who had been following the auction online and wanted my assistance in obtaining a horse she wanted to rescue. She gave me the tag number and a brief description of this horse and asked if I had seen him there. I turned and quickly scanned the room, looking for this mystery horse she was talking about. I couldn't believe my eyes when I saw him standing just two horses down from the sorrel gelding! He was a beautiful brown and white paint gelding with a star on his forehead, and he appeared to stand about the same height as the sorrel horse.

We talked about a plan for how I would obtain this horse, and she assured me that the money would be deposited into my account to pay for him. After I located the dealer who owned the paint and finalized his purchase, I then returned to the first dealer, determined to seal the deal with him and get the sorrel gelding to safety. As I approached this ruthless man once again, I glanced over at the copper-colored horse and quietly studied him for a few minutes. It was difficult to ignore his bold and brave stature as he stood quietly among the other horses. Amidst the loud, unfamiliar noises and confusion he never faltered, but stood firm and strong, unmoving in his stance, with head held high. Watching him reminded me of a courageous Indian chief, standing atop a high mountain cliff, arms crossed in front of him as he looks down on his tribe in the valley below; always watching, always protecting, and never giving in to fear. I knew then, in that instant, what his name would be, and from that moment on he was called "Chief."

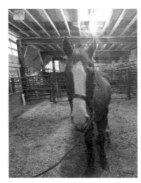

Chief, at the auction barn

Chapter 9

Hope Restored for Chief

Isaiah 59:1

Sin, Confession and Redemption

"Surely the arm of the Lord is not too short to save, nor his ear too dull to hear" (**New International Version**).

Chief spent the next several months at Keirstin's farm, under the close observation and expertise of the barn manager, Bethany.

He spent two months in quarantine, receiving lots of nutritious food as well as vet, farrier, and dental care, and the remainder of springtime grazing in the open green pastures, regaining his strength and just enjoying being a horse again.

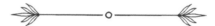

The arrival of summer brought new promise and hope for us all, and by mid-August we prepared to bring Chief home to our farm. The morning began like all others, in that I awoke early to get the barn work done so we could be on our way. We expected the trip to Keirstin's farm to be approximately an hour and a half, one way—three hours, round trip—not including any needed stops along the way. Knowing this, we figured the whole trip would take up most of our day, so we wanted to get an early start. Once my husband, Steve, got the trailer hooked up, he met me at the barn and we were on our way. Surprisingly, I found myself quite excited about this particular trip. It was not a common practice for Steve and I to take trips like this one together. Typically, he used the trailer to haul cattle, and rarely horses. But I was glad to have this unique opportunity with him, away from the busyness of daily farm life. Ironically, today presented the perfect opportunity for Steve to get a real glimpse into some of the "behind-the-scenes" work that is required with these special rescue horses. Looking back, I realize that this day may have been the turning point that opened his eyes and heart to this special mission.

When we arrived at Keirstin's, we met up with Bethany, who gave us important updates on Chief. She explained everything they had done for him during his six-month stay, and how she and her husband had grown quite fond of him. Ultimately, they had hoped to adopt him for her husband and young son, but their current living situation wouldn't allow it. They really hated to see him leave. As she turned and walked up the hill to retrieve Chief from the pasture, I felt an overwhelming sadness for her. I knew what it was like to grow very attached to a horse, only to have to let them go months later. It seemed to take an extra-long time before Bethany returned with Chief. When she did appear over the hill, her slow and purposeful walk told me everything; I knew she had been taking the much-needed time to say her good-byes in private. Once Chief was loaded onto the trailer and Steve climbed back into the truck, I gave Bethany a big ol' hug and assured her we would take excellent care of him and give her regular updates. After thanking her for everything she had done for Chief and myself, I jumped into the truck, quickly swiping away my tears as we drove down the driveway and out of sight.

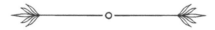

Once Chief got settled in, we set up a schedule for a trainer to work with him and do riding evaluations. The next thing on the "to-do" list was to advertise him as available for adoption.

Chief did not stay with us for long. Shortly after he arrived, I received a message from a young girl who saw his ad for adoption and "felt drawn to him" and asked if she could come see him the following Monday. When she arrived, I instantly felt she was the perfect fit for Chief. She was so sweet and soft-spoken; I loved how patient she was as she handled him so calmly and gently. When she rode him around the farm, I could see that he responded very well to her, and apparently, she felt the same way too. It was a bittersweet encounter that ended on a good note, because Chief left our farm that day to begin his new life with Sara. Since his departure, I have visited Chief and Sara several times and am constantly amazed at his incredible progress. Through Sara's loving care and guidance, they have forged an incredible and inseparable relationship and have bonded like no others I have ever seen. Every time I visit with them, I feel so encouraged by what I see, and I leave feeling so blessed. Blessed, because through this incredible pairing, I too have forged a wonderful friendship with Sara.

Chief, at his new home with Sara.

Chapter 10

Cupid's Special Gift

John 14:27

"Peace I leave with you; my peace I give you. I do not give to you as the world gives. Do not let your hearts be troubled and do not be afraid" (New International Version).

It was a normal day in February, and it started out like any other, but it ended in a very life-changing way. It was Monday morning, and my friend Lori and I were on our way to a nearby auction house, a place that has become a regular stomping ground for us. We decided to go there that day "just to look." Plus, Lori had said she wanted to buy a saddle for Hope. We should have known better from our past experiences—we rarely showed up at the auction and left empty-handed. Point proven: just months earlier there was Peppy personality, who had reached out through the metal gate and touched my heart forever. Then, a few months later, I found Hope standing among all the aisles of other desolate auction horses. In much the same way, and just last month, Chief had entered my life and was now with his forever family.

As we entered the auction house, I was surprised to notice how packed it was for February. Usually, the mid-winter months bring a decline in the number of horses that go through the auction, but today was different. As we walked around looking at all the horses, Lori noticed this tall, grey gelding standing in the east wing. He was a beautiful grey horse with a dark mane and tail. He looked like a fancy show horse, and I wondered what could have happened in his life to land him here. After Lori spent some time with the handsome grey, we continued our walk around the barn, carefully taking in every detail about each horse that we leisurely strode past.

Then, I saw her. She stood alone, tied to a post in a single stall on the opposite side of the barn from where the grey gelding stood. She was the prettiest-looking rose grey, flea-bitten grey mare I had ever seen. She was clean and well-groomed, and her mane was carefully braided from top to bottom. There was a scar on her right front leg that ran from below her knee to above her hoof, leaving me to wonder what this poor, sweet mare had endured in her life. I noticed what appeared to be the faint outline of a freeze brand that marked her left hip, revealing the distinct lines of the letter "R."

Cali at the auction barn, before being rescued.

Someone must have really loved and cared for her, I thought. What tragedy could have happened in a person's life to drive them to sell their beloved horse? Were they even aware that their precious horse was sitting in an auction house, in grave danger of being bought by a dealer and ultimately shipped to slaughter? These were the questions that haunted my mind constantly, leaving me to wonder if I would ever know the real stories behind these poor, debilitated, and desperate horses.

As I was pondering over these questions, some men came over, threw a bridle and saddle on her, and led her toward the auction ring. As I watched her go through the sale, she appeared to be struggling, yet still tried to do whatever her rider was asking of her. She was such a pretty horse, I was sure she would attract a private buyer and end up in a good home. However, to my dismay, she was not sold. As we weaved our way back through the barn, I found the grey mare tied in a small stall underneath the bleachers. A tall, grisly-looking man was preparing to leave the stall, so I approached him and asked if he was the owner and what he was planning to do with her. "Oh, I'll take her to another sale until she sells, and if she doesn't sell, I guess she'll head to Mexico." At that moment, I walked over to her and touched her face. Such a pretty, dainty face, but it was obvious to me that she wasn't doing well. Her eyes, appearing droopy and very tired, were void of any light and held an emptiness within them. Lord knows how many auctions she had been through before today, and I had a strong feeling that she would not survive another one. As she stood there with her head hung down, I felt the all-too-familiar tug on my heart. A tug that I always had a difficult time ignoring—the same strong desire that had led me to rescue the previous horses.

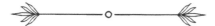

I joined up with Lori again, and as we walked in search of the dealers, we discussed our options and devised a plan. If we had any doubts about helping these two grey horses, they were quickly extinguished with what happened next: as we stood in the middle of the aisleway talking with one of the dealers, I turned to see both grey horses walking through the crowd toward us. When they finally reached us, they stopped and stood quietly beside us. Somehow, they had gotten loose, and it was almost as if they were searching for us. Well, that did it for me. We took the horses to an area of the barn where we could tie them together, re-located the dealers, and finalized the transaction. I then contacted Bethany to set up transportation and quarantine.

We spent the next hour getting acquainted with our two new rescue horses and making sure they were comfortable and had plenty to eat and drink. As I rubbed the grey mare's neck, I lifted her cream-colored mane and noticed a small red marking that looked like a rose.

I thought of Valentine's Day and the red rose of California. The rose of California is one of the prettiest and most carefree plants. It is a typical "rose" with short leaves, thorns, and flowers on the long stems. They are best known for their lovely fragrance. The hips of the rose (seed-bearing fruit) are bright red and rich in medicinal and curative properties. As I considered the perfect name for this sweet, frail-looking, rose grey mare, suddenly it hit me, and there was no doubt in my mind. Her name would be Cali. *Cali*, I thought to myself, *you are Cupid's special gift, and someday you will make a special young girl extremely happy.*

The grey gelding that Lori rescued came to be known as Stormy. Because, Lori said, "his coloring looks like a storm cloud, and I believe he has endured many storms in his life."

Chapter 11

A New Home for Cali

1 Chronicles 17:9

"And I will provide a place for my people Israel and will plant them so that they can have a home of their own and no longer be disturbed. Wicked people will not oppress them anymore, as they did at the beginning" (New International Version).

Over the next thirty days, Cali and Stormy spent their time recovering at Keirstin's quarantine. It was a long, stressful month full of uncertainty, beginning the morning that I received a desperate phone call from Keirstin. Cali had been with them less than forty-eight hours when I got the call. "Cali is not doing well," she quickly blurted out. "She went down early this morning and has been really struggling. Bethany was able to get her up and has been walking her around all morning, trying to keep her on her feet." With bated breath, I quietly listened as Keirstin frantically continued: "We called the vet, and they are on their way. I will let you know how she's doing after the vet examines her." And with that, she ended the call.

Needless to say, I was a complete bundle of nerves while waiting for the call back from Keirstin. It seemed like forever till I heard from her. But then, the phone finally rang. Gripping the receiver with white-knuckled anticipation, I held my breath, waiting for the dreaded report. "Cali is going to be okay, at least for now," she blurted out. "The vet gave her lots of fluids, electrolytes, and antibiotics. He wants us to watch her closely for the next few days, especially since she was so severely dehydrated, she will be at greater risk for colic. And in her weakened and exhausted state, chances are higher that she could go down again."

Fortunately, Cali pulled through that nail-biting event and has been going strong ever since. She had been diagnosed with shipping fever, and had most likely picked it up from being at multiple auctions and transported long distances. One thing I learned from Cali during this time is that she is a survivor and a fighter. The scar on her front right leg was evidence of that.

A week after Cali's scary episode, Lori and I went to visit her and Stormy at the quarantine. As we were walking them around outside, allowing them to graze on the nice, green grass, Lori exclaimed, "Look at Stormy—he's walking kinda funny." Sure enough, as I watched him walk away from me, his back legs, appearing quite wobbly, would give out on him every few steps he took. It almost seemed like he could not hold his weight on his back end.

This simple observation kicked off a torrent of vet visits, blood work, and more tests. In the end, it was discovered that Stormy had EPM (equine protozoal myeloencephalitis). Apparently, according to test results and vet determination, the disease was in the late stages, and there wasn't much to offer him in conservative or affordable treatment. Unfortunately, the treatment that was an option for him was very costly and offered no guarantee of improvement. This forced Lori to make a very difficult decision—one that left her in complete turmoil. In the end, she grasped at the hope that any treatment would make a difference. So, when quarantine was completed, she made plans to move him to a boarding stable near her home so she could keep a closer eye on him.

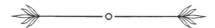

It was mid-March on a Sunday afternoon when Lori and the stable owner, Jim, drove to Keirstin's farm with his horse trailer in tow. I had made plans with them a few days earlier, suggesting my intent to board Cali at the same stable for a couple of months until she got adopted out. So, the two of them drove to the quarantine with the intent of bringing three horses back with them.

It had turned colder and was snowing heavily. To make matters worse, the horses were in the pasture and did not want to be caught.

After two long hours of running and chasing horses through the thick, muddy pastures, the cold, drenched, and mud-covered buckaroos finally rounded up the defiant horses, loaded them onto the trailer, and were heading to the stable in Felton, PA.

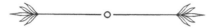

I did not get to see Cali until a few days later but was welcomed by her excited whinny as I approached her stall. She had already become a favorite among the other boarders in the barn, and before long, it was easy to see why. She was such a sweet, spunky, and comical horse. One thing in particular that I often witnessed her doing was that she'd push her stall door open immediately after it was unlatched. She was always quick to greet you at the front of her stall and would abruptly yank the door open, eager to walk out with you and see the world.

It did not take long for Cali's unique beauty and sweetness to be noticed, and within two months a man inquired about adopting her for his young daughter. His daughter, Helen, had a special love of horses and had formed a very close bond with Cali.

Cali after completing quarantine, before being adopted.

It was an unforgettable night when the adoption of Cali became official. The stable owner held a country-style Memorial Day cookout, complete with a table full of wholesome home-cooked food, and finished off with a huge bonfire situated in the middle of the arena.

The look on Helen's face when her dad presented her with Cali was absolutely priceless. It was so good to see the sparkle return to this young girl's troubled eyes, and her ear-to-ear smile. After the formalities were done and I turned to leave, I heard Helen muttering to herself the many different names she could think of for Cali, attempting to come up with the perfect one.

As I drove down the stone driveway and turned onto the road, heading away from the stable, I wondered where Cali's life would be in a year or two. I truly hoped things would work out for her.

Periodically, Helen would send me pictures of her and Cali, whom she now referred to as "Freckles." They seemed happy and had adjusted well to each other. Helen was excited to tell me about the young filly her dad had bought for her to raise and train. We kept in contact for the next year and a half, and then all of a sudden, all correspondence from Helen came to a halt.

Chapter 12

My Blue-Eyed Gentleman

Philippians 4:5

"Let your gentleness be evident to all. The Lord is near" (New International Version).

It was Monday, March 17, 2017, and I found myself at the local horse auction once again. Melanie, my contact for the auction, had messaged me earlier that morning, asking if I was going to the horse auction and if I could proxy bid for a couple of ladies who lived out of state. I immediately said I'd be happy to do this and quickly wrote down all the needed info.

As I walked through the huge double doors and into the sale barn, I quickly weaved my way through the multiple aisles of horses, scanning and assessing the horses closely for the ones I'd be bidding on. One lady was looking for a blind, aged Cremello gelding. She wanted to save this horse which she was certain would head to slaughter. The other lady I had spoken to on the phone just minutes earlier stated that she wanted to "help save as many horses as possible, no specific requirements." Armed with this information, I picked up my pace, determined to find these horses before the auction began. In the past, I'd seen many horses get lost to prospective private buyers because they didn't watch them closely enough, and they disappeared into thin air.

As I weaved my way through the aisles of the barn, I was about to give up all hope of finding the requested horses when suddenly, as I walked into the east side of the building, I saw him standing amongst a cluster of other horses. The Cremello gelding stood quietly between two other horses, methodically munching away on his hay. The milky cloudiness that filled his eyes made it obvious that he was blind. But as I approached him, he did not appear startled at all by my presence. He was so calm and friendly, such a beautiful, sweet soul.

As I glanced around at the other horses standing in the same aisleway as the Cremello, I noticed a young filly. Guessing from her size, it was highly probable that she had just recently been weaned from her mother. The poor little thing looked terrified in this strange, cold environment and was frantically searching for her mama. I determined right then and there that I would try my best to help her out of this horrifying situation.

After studying the other horses in the immediate area, I found an aged pinto gelding and a sorrel mare. I quickly placed another phone call to the two ladies to report my findings and confirm their intentions. I then moved on to complete the purchases with the dealer and arrange transport to their new homes. As I was wrapping up the details and preparing to leave, my eyes fell on a horse standing next to the dealer. He was a sorrel paint gelding with a bald face and one blue eye. As I persistently tried to avoid contact with him, I told myself, *I just bought four horses for two ladies; I can't afford to take on another one right now.* However, the more I tried to ignore him, the more persistent he was in getting my attention. His final attempt to win my heart began with him nudging my arm and ended with him softly laying his head on my shoulder. This not-so-subtle attempt at recognition did not go unnoticed, and I fell victim to saving yet one more horse that day.

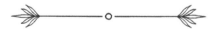

As I left the auction barn and headed to the parking lot, I felt completely overwhelmed by two conflicting emotions. On one hand, I was feeling total elation and victory for the horses I was able to step in and help that day. On the other hand, I couldn't help but feel like I had failed all the other poor souls still standing in the barn behind me—those who were either bought by kill buyers, dealers, or flippers, and were fearfully waiting to be loaded onto the huge stock trailers. *I will never get used to this feeling,* I thought to myself. With tears streaming down my face and a sick feeling in the pit of my stomach, I climbed into my car and drove toward the quarantine facility which would be the temporary home for this blue-eyed gentleman now known as Sage, feeling some comfort in knowing that at least these five horses I had helped today would now have a second chance at a new life.

Chapter 13

Sage's Purpose

Job 42:2

"I know that you can do all things; no purpose of yours can be thwarted" (New International Version).

One of God's special creations—the horse, each one gifted with their own unique personality traits—was made with a specific purpose in mind: God's purpose.

Sage, with his one blue eye and gentle-like nature, immediately attracts and draws people to him. His cautious demeanor mirrors that of the timid, even fearful emotions of hurting kids. Often, once an initial bond is felt and a connection is made, Sage offers up the best hugs I've ever experienced. This simple act of kindness is what initiates the journey of healing for a hurting child.

Sage, at our farm-June 2017

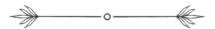

Little did I know at the time of Sage's rescue, or that of any of our rescued horses, the profound impact they would make in the hearts and lives of children, as well as families and volunteers.

The first youths to walk onto our property arrived disheveled and unsure. *What brought them here?* I wondered, as I welcomed them and gave a quick tour of the barn and introduced the horses. "Well, it's the horses," they replied in unison. "We noticed them driving by with our family and wanted to stop and see them." What began as curiosity quickly turned into a weekly session with these two lost girls, searching for answers.

Interestingly, the girl who was having difficulty dealing with an absent father and a mother who worked all the time felt drawn to Sage. During one of her sessions, as she stood quietly grooming Sage, talking softly, her emotions just spilled out. It was at this moment that I saw Sage reach around her with his head and give her a big ol' hug. The transformation I witnessed on this young girl's face was remarkable. I saw the tension and anger melt away, replaced with a look of reverence and peace. These young, troubled girls faithfully showed up once a week for a few months, then one day, they suddenly stopped coming. From time to time, they would reach out and ask about the horses while relaying information about their well-being. They both loved the horses and enjoyed their weekly visits, but life and responsibilities were getting in the way.

One thing I have realized over the years: as terrific as horses are, they were not made to be the ever-present solution to everyone's problems.

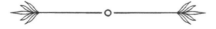

Fast forward to one year and three months later: Sage was all settled in at Hope's Haven and ready to continue living out his second purpose in life—his God-given purpose.

Our first season in operation as a 501(c)(3) non-profit was June-October of 2018. As we prepared to host our first annual kick-off chicken barbeque, little did we know just how much our then-three program horses (Rita, Hope, and Sage) would impact the lives of hurting children and their families forever.

The first family arrived one evening for a simple meet-and-greet with the horses. After introductions were made, the three young boys and their mother were slowly led down the aisle of the barn. One by one, as we passed in front of the stalls, I purposefully relayed each horse's story. "Every horse has a story—a history, just like people do," I explained. "And unfortunately, most stories of rescue horses are not happy ones."

When we stopped in front of Sage's stall and I finished telling his story, I heard three young voices say in disbelief, "How could anyone get rid of him? He's so beautiful."

Of course, they all wanted to get a closer look at him, so I quickly put on his halter, snapped on his lead, and positioned him between his cross ties. As Sage stood quietly in the aisleway, the middle boy slowly raised his hand and gently touched Sage's nose. "You wanna know something really cool?" the young boy asked. "Sage's right eye is blue, and my right eye has a birthmark in it." Ironically, it was these two small yet significant details that connected boy and horse for the next couple of years. From that day forward, Sage and Landon had a very special bond. A bond that began with a common story, and two identifiable marks.

I later learned that Landon's father had not been involved with him for much of his life, and for the most part has been non-existent to this day. It was very apparent that this absence had caused a very deep and real hurt that was felt by him every day.

This young boy's story was practically identical to Sage's story, in which his former owner, a teenage boy, had become so busy with other interests that he no longer had time for Sage. This fact eventually led the boy's parents to sell him and his two pasture mates to a horse dealer, which consequently landed him at the auction house, into my life, and therefore into Hope's Haven.

Throughout the summer, Landon and Sage formed a very strong

connection. This boy, who first appeared at Hope's Haven shy, timid, and extremely fearful of horses, was riding bareback on Sage by the end of the season.

In fact, their relationship was so remarkable and made such an impact on me that the original Hope's Haven logo was initially created using Sage and Landon at the heart of it. The logo, a shadow of a young boy hugging his newfound friend, Sage, remains a constant reminder to me of the inseparable bond formed between a hurting boy and a lost horse named Sage.

Chapter 14

Our Trip to Oregon

Hebrews 11:1

"Now faith is confidence in what we hope for and assurance about what we do not see" (New International Version).

It was May of 2017 when I boarded a plane bound for Oregon with my daughter Kristin. We were so excited to take this trip together and looked forward to experiencing the beautiful, rugged outdoors, complemented by the majestic, snow-covered Cascade Range mountains. I remember reading all about the beauty surrounding Bend, Oregon, in the many inspiring books written by Kim Meeder, founder of Crystal Peaks Youth Ranch.

As we settled into our seats waiting for the plane to take off, I couldn't believe that in less than twenty-four hours I would be meeting the two people I had admired from afar for so many years. For as long as I could remember, I had always felt a desire to start up a horse rescue program that also helped at-risk youth. Many years ago, I had learned of Kim and Troy Meeder's program and was in complete awe, following what they were doing from afar. Now, the moment had finally arrived, and I was "over-the moon" excited to have this opportunity to attend one of their IGNITION clinics and learn how to start up a similar ministry.

After our plane landed at Redmond airport, we grabbed our luggage, found our rental car, and headed out for our first adventure in Oregon. Since the IGNITION clinic was scheduled to begin the next day, this gave us the rest of the afternoon and evening to take in all of the beautiful sights in and around the neighboring towns. Our first stop was the quaint village town of Sisters, Oregon. I later learned that this charming little town had earned its name from the Three Sisters Cascade Range mountains situated over the town. As we drove toward our destination, the total splendor of the mountains looming before us was absolutely breathtaking; I knew this was going to be a special visit. With its 1880s Wild West ambience, Sisters offers everything from authentic, saloon-style eateries to vibrant art galleries and boutiques. This town definitely had my seal of approval for having the most wholesome and family-friendly appeal.

After enjoying a delicious lunch at the Sisters Saloon and Ranch Grill, we took a stroll around town and casually browsed through some of the neighboring shops. We wrapped up our visit to this beautiful town after buying some popular wine from a local shop called The Gallimaufry. Reluctantly, we then headed back to our car and turned toward the small town of Redmond, where our hotel awaited us.

After settling into our hotel, we set out on another adventurous excursion. This time we headed for the much bigger, more populated city of Bend. As we drove into the city, I was completely mesmerized by the beauty of the surrounding area. With towering pine trees dotting the perimeter of Bend and the majestic Cascade mountains in the backdrop, it was like nothing I had ever seen before.

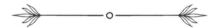

Bend, Oregon, is best known for its attractive, friendly, and social atmosphere, offering numerous activities for the whole family to enjoy, including craft breweries, coffee shops, unique restaurants, breathtaking scenery, and the usual, local events. Amongst these highlights are also a myriad of exciting outdoor activities to suit everyone's taste. There are numerous hiking trails, mountain biking, skiing, rock climbing, and paragliding, to name a few.

After we parked our car, we began our visit by taking a relaxing stroll through the Deschutes River Park. This unique attraction is home to Bend's most adventurous water sports. With the popular Deschutes River flowing through the heart of Bend's Old Mill district, it offers the perfect location for both adrenaline-filled and family-friendly activities. Whatever you're in the mood for, the Deschutes River Park offers it all. If you're looking for a more tranquil experience, you can choose to leisurely float down the river or hop in a paddle boat or kayak. Or, if you're a thrill-seeker craving an adrenaline rush, the Deschutes River also offers whitewater activities such as body boarding, surfing, or rafting.

We were in no hurry as we meandered around this fun-filled park, watching folks enjoying life and taking in the whole carefree atmosphere. How I wished life back home could be this carefree and un-hurried. I knew there was something very special about Bend, Oregon. Maybe it was the friendly, medicinal atmosphere—breathing in the crisp, clean mountain air—or just the mere fact that I felt called here. I definitely knew this was where God had placed me at this time in my life.

Later, as we continued our journey uptown toward the beer distillery, I was shocked once again by the mere politeness of the locals. Unlike in the east coast cities back home, the pedestrians who confidently walked the streets of Bend appeared unaffected by the fact that they had the right of way when crossing the streets. Instead of hearing cars gunning their engines in an attempt to race past the unsuspecting pedestrian emerging onto the crosswalks, these local city folks of Bend literally screeched their tires as they slammed on the brakes to allow us tourists to safely cross the street. I was totally amazed by this genuine act of (un-hurried) courtesy. It is unfortunate these days that this simple act of kindness is rarely seen anymore.

After touring the distillery and purchasing some souvenirs of t-shirts and coffee mugs, we headed downtown to investigate the city of Bend and to find a local restaurant to grab some dinner. We settled for a popular bar and grill off Main Street, and it did not disappoint—both the food and the service were outstanding.

With full stomachs and adventurous hearts, we headed back to our hotel to catch a good night's sleep before the long-awaited day when we'd finally meet Kim and Troy Meeder and see their lovely ranch. I was so excited I could barely sleep, thinking about the surrealness of it all. I mean, what were the possibilities that I would be living out the very thing I had dreamed about since I was a kid? The *one* thing I had always felt was God's purpose for my life was actually unfolding in front of me, one piece at a time.

Chapter 15

The Nuts and Bolts of Horse Ministry

2 Corinthians 3:3

"You show that you are a letter from Christ, the result of our ministry, written not with ink but with the Spirit of the living God, not on tablets of stone but on tablets of human hearts" (New International Version).

Dawn broke early the next morning as I was rudely awakened by my alarm at 5:30 a.m. I could barely control myself as my feet hit the cold floor, and I rushed around the room in a frenzy to get ready. Miraculously, we both managed to shower, dress, and get out the door in just under thirty minutes. Anxious to grab breakfast before heading to the ranch, we quickly shuffled through the parking lot to where the hotel's modest continental breakfast awaited.

After stuffing ourselves full of biscuits n' gravy, we packed into the car and headed north toward the Three Sisters mountains and Crystal Peaks Youth Ranch.

As we casually drove to our destination, we purposefully took our time to breathe in all of the beautiful scenery around us. No matter which direction we turned or which road we took, the Three Sisters mountains somehow magically appeared to our left. It was as if they were guiding us through our mysterious journey north as we headed deeper into nature and closer to the ranch.

As we pulled into the parking area across the road from Crystal Peaks, we were delighted to see guests being transported to the clinic site on the back of four-wheeled gators and a red classic Ford pick-up truck.

After checking in at the ranch office we hiked up the infamous long stone driveway, lined with beautiful pine trees and colorful flower beds. On either side of the driveway were the horse pastures, filled with the many notable rescue and program horses I had read about in Kim's first two books, *Hope Rising* and *A Bridge Called*

Hope. I found myself wondering if Hero was one of the horses in the surrounding pastures. Hero, as I had learned years ago, was one of Crystal Peaks' special rescue horses. After fully recovering from a horrific injury that had left him without his left eye, he became one of their biggest ambassadors for hurting kids. I hoped I'd have the opportunity to see him. After reading about his unfortunate situation and harrowing rescue in *Fierce Beauty*, I chose to sponsor him with a one-time donation toward his recovery. I felt as though I already knew this very special "hero" of a horse.

Entrance to Crystal Peaks Youth Ranch, and the infamous long, stone driveway, May 2017

Me and Kristin on the back of the classic ford pick up.

As we rounded the final turn and walked toward the ranch, we were suddenly captivated by the awe-inspiring beauty that lay before us. Sitting in the distance behind the ranch, amidst the vast acreage of green pine trees, were the snow-capped peaks of the Three Sisters mountains—pure, unspoiled nature at its best.

As we settled around the main building for the meet-and-greet, I watched as the growing crowd of newly arrived guests swarmed in. It was so easy to feel welcome amongst all these strangers when surrounded by such genuine, down-home country folk; I was so amazed to learn all the different geographical locations the guests had traveled from. There were families from Washington State; couples from California, Colorado, and Virginia; people from Pennsylvania and as far north as Maine.

After all the formalities were done, Kim and Troy took us on a tour of Crystal Peaks, describing the intimate details of its unique history, or their "Cinderella" story. We then gathered in front of a small corral behind the main building for introductions to some of their program horses. It was here that I met Hero for the first time. As the horses were being walked around the corral in front of us, I spotted the small bay gelding coming toward me. When his leader stopped in front of me, Hero turned toward me and gently touched my hand with his nose. What an awesome feeling that was, to meet the horse I had read about in Kim's book! The attachment that was formed purely from his story of pain and redemption was like nothing I had ever experienced.

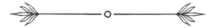

Afterward, everyone was ushered into the large meeting room for the first session—introduction to ranch staff and fellowship with Kim and Troy. This was the first day of four intensely packed days of lectures, demonstrations, and clinics; a huge preparatory clinic for those traveling from afar in hopes of learning everything they needed to start up a similar ministry, akin to Crystal Peaks. Once the ranch staff completed their introductions, Troy spoke in depth on how to develop your ministry's vision, mission statement, and values. Never in my life could I have imagined just how much was involved in starting a 501(c)(3) non-profit ministry. Yet Crystal Peaks is where my journey began, and it was the beginning of a very challenging and multi-dimensional journey. A journey in which I felt strongly that these two mentors standing before me would always be there to guide me along the rocky paths leading to and through my ministry. In fact, it was during this particular lecture that the name "Hope's Haven Rescue and Youth Camp" was developed and our mission statement created: "To rescue equines, mentor children, restore hope, and re-home equines to 4ever homes 4life."

Kim and Troy were everything I had imagined them to be: genuine, wholesome, God-fearing people who also happened to be excellent speakers. Troy was the true definition of the boy next door, and just as approachable and easy to talk to; and Kim, with her bubbly, charismatic personality and honest, back-to-nature demeanor made everyone instantly like them and feel as if we had known them our whole life.

As they rolled through their explanation of what would be covered over the next few days, it was easy to see the deep-rooted passion they felt for this wonderful ministry.

The day was filled to the brim with valuable information, equipping all those in attendance with the knowledge needed for them to methodically place in their tool box—the "nuts and bolts" of horse ministry do's and don'ts. By the time the dinner bell rang, everyone looked famished and on mental overload. Fortunately, our two warm hosts knew exactly how to serve up a grand dinner, and they did so with country flair—a fully catered meal with all the fixings you could possibly want, served on the front porch overlooking the picturesque Cascade Range mountains. What a perfect way to complement this most enriching and glorious day.

Chapter 16

The Hill, the Cross, and a Sign

Philippians 1:6

"Being confident of this, that he who began a good work in you will carry it on to completion until the day of Christ Jesus" (New International Version).

The second day was just as intense as the first. It began with Pastor Troy's invigorating fellowship that only renewed and replenished our spirits, preparing us for another day of horse ministry education. One of the key points Troy mentioned has stuck with me to this day: "Mission work isn't where you go, it's where you are—the ground where you are standing every day." This simple yet profound truth has unfolded before my very eyes every day since. If we keep our hearts open, we can see so many opportunities to serve, right in our own back yard.

The early morning was bustling with activity as we attended demo clinics on TRU horsemanship, a type of horse/human relationship which is primarily built on Trust, Respect, and Understanding. This is especially important when working with rescue horses that have formerly experienced mistreatment of any kind by their former owner(s). **Trust** needs to be rebuilt and can be a long process. Rescue horses need to learn that they can trust humans, and that no harm will ever come to them by way of their current owner, or mankind, ever again. **Respect** is a two-way street; it goes hand-in-hand with trust and is a necessity when working with any horse, especially rescue horses. If a horse doesn't trust you, he won't respect you—and chances are, you will get hurt. **Understanding** is a vital part of this relationship as well, because in order to get a horse to do what you want him to do, he first needs to understand what it is you are asking of him, and you need to understand why he reacts the way he does.

By mid-morning, we had switched gears and were involved in educational lectures related to volunteer programming and herd management. I felt as if I was back in college, toting around my thick binder and all my assorted pens, eagerly taking notes in my feeble attempt to retain all of this valuable information. The morning ended with another fabulous catered lunch served on the back deck, complete with all the fixings, to refuel our energy.

The afternoon introduced us to the more sensitive topics, such as: "The Heart and Soul of the Ministry"; "The Kids"; "Beginning a Non-Profit: Administration, Insurance"; and "Shielding Your Ministry—Weighing the Risk, Protecting the Ministry." We then wrapped up the day with a nice stroll to the top of "the Hill" for a time of quiet reflection and prayer. I found this to be a true revelation, after a full day of attempting to digest all of the detailed information received from Troy.

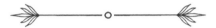

The Hill was the tallest point on the ranch property. It overlooked what used the be the cinder pit that Crystal Peaks was built on twenty-five years ago. It was during this time of quiet meditation that I fervently sought God's guidance once again. Even though I had always felt in my heart that horse ministry was what God had called me to do, I needed one more push—a sign from above—to convince me of that.

The Cross on the Hill at Crystal Peaks Youth Ranch

My prayer sounded something like this: "Dear Lord, I feel in my heart that this is what You've called me to do, but can You give me one definite sign to prove beyond a doubt that this is what I'm to be doing?"

I did not have to wait long for the miraculous sign from above to be revealed to me. As I sat, Indian- style, on the ground beside the cross, my eyes fell on a most wondrous sight: this tall, strong-structured woman kneeling in the tall grass just below and to the right of the cross was Kim. She appeared to be so entranced in her profound fellowship with her heavenly Father that everything around her was tuned out; it was just herself and God. I found myself wondering if I could ever have such a deep and real relationship with God.

In that very moment, the dark, thick clouds that had hung above us broke away, revealing the bright, radiant sun. It was as if the heavens were proclaiming, "Yes, yes, yes! This is exactly what I've called you to do."

Unconvinced, as a dense cluster of dark clouds again blocked the sun from my view, my stubborn heart once again asked God to reveal a sign. This time it took only a few seconds for the Almighty to reveal His answer. As if the Holy Spirit Himself was pulling back the curtain and extinguishing my doubt, the clouds parted, and the bright sun broke through again. This time it made a grander entrance; the sight was truly amazing as the sun's rays stretched across the sky above us. I could almost hear the heavenly hosts singing, "Hallelujah! Now get up on your feet and go forth into your ministry. Tell the good news of Jesus to the children. This is your calling."

And get up is what I did. I jumped up off the ground, straightened myself up, dusted the dirt from my pants, and with a huge smile on my face, headed down the hill and back to the ranch. I knew now beyond a doubt what I must do.

Chapter 17

My Calling

Jeremiah 32:19

"Great are your purposes and mighty are your deeds. Your eyes are open to the ways of all mankind; you reward each person according to their conduct and as their deeds deserve" (New International Version).

The all-revealing experience on the Hill completely filled me with inspiration and a whole new purpose. God's powerful interaction and message left me with no doubt as to what He was calling me to do. Make no mistake about it—He has brought us all to this marvelous place for a reason, to fulfill His divine and infinite plan. It reminded me of the many disciples and missionaries who are called to go forth into the world and preach the Gospel. In much the same way, the people gathered at Crystal Peaks for this IGNITION clinic were also representative of this same calling, forming an elite army for Christ by setting up our own ministry camps in the backyards of our hometowns. I remember a day when Troy was describing their "similar ministry" program. Since the launching of this program several years ago, they have helped to start up and mentor over 200 similar ministries throughout the United States, as well as in other countries. To be accepted as an "official" similar ministry of Crystal Peaks, there are numerous requirements one needs to fulfill, with the most important being that it is a faith-based ministry in which the redeeming love of Jesus is the foundation of everything we do. This is especially important, since as a "similar ministry" we are modeling after Crystal Peaks, and everything we do reflects Jesus' love for the broken-hearted. As I sat listening to Troy describe this unique community, I couldn't help but ponder, *Maybe someday my ministry will be a part of this remarkable community, where everyone is connected in the same purpose, sharing in the likeness of their own mission and vision to serve Christ above all else.* I couldn't imagine a better group to be affiliated with.

At the close of the day, we all said our farewells, promising to see each other the next morning. Then we headed down the driveway to locate our cars, to head back to town and onward to our next adventure.

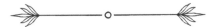

That evening, Kristin and I decided to take in more of the sights and sounds of Bend. We found a parking area centrally located in the city. Suddenly realizing how hungry we were after our long, activity-filled day, we proceeded to locate an eatery we both could agree on. We settled for a cute but cozy-looking bar and grill right off of Main Street. We were so happy we did, because the food was excellent and the service just as good. As I sat there enjoying the delicious food and unique atmosphere of this city, it became very clear to me that Bend was definitely in a category all its own.

After dinner, we took a stroll through different sections of the city, stopping at a few local shops and pubs along the way, browsing for that one special souvenir, distinctive only to Bend.

I believe we made new friends everywhere we stopped. There was just something special about Bend that resonated genuine friendliness among the locals, and we especially loved the fun, friendly atmosphere.

The next morning, as I awoke to get ready for our third clinic day, Kristin announced that she wasn't feeling well and decided to stay behind at the hotel. Hesitantly, I finished getting ready, checked to make sure she was okay, then headed off to have breakfast on my own.

As I took my seat for morning fellowship with pastor Troy, I felt so refreshed and inspired to learn everything I could. I wanted to start my ministry out on the right foot and give it my entire heart and soul. After yesterday's all-revealing and inspirational moment with God on the Hill, it was utterly impossible for me to deny the powerful feeling of direction He had given me. I had walked away and down the Hill completely satiated in His will. And now, sitting here amongst nearly a hundred people, all with similar goals and paths before them, I knew I was taking the right road—for the first time in my life, it was His direction.

That day was just like the first, in that we were on the receiving end of so much valuable information, all the while surrounded by a genuinely warm, family-like atmosphere. Looking around the room at everyone, it was so easy to get caught up in the excitement as we all sat in anticipation of what Troy was going to teach us next.

Among the many topics covered that morning were part two of TRU Horsemanship, and Structured Chaos, or Hoof Care. After another delicious lunch served on the back deck, the afternoon's agenda involved such topics as Correcting Common Mistakes; Sample Sessions in Horse and Child Safety; Creativity in Sessions; and Vet Care; after a much-needed break, Troy wrapped up the day with valuable information on fundraising, followed by a Q&A session with the staff.

Friday evening wrapped up beautifully with a huge, cowboy-style BBQ, with genuine angus beef burgers and hot dogs cooked over a roaring fire and served up with a warm, friendly smile. As ranch guests sat around the fire, swapping ministry stories and roasting marshmallows, the cowboys (male staff) played their guitars and sang songs. It was such an authentic western atmosphere, I swore I could hear the coyotes howling in the distance.

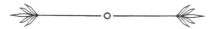

By the time I arrived back at our hotel, Kristin was more than ready to be released from her eight hours of captivity and anxious to flee from the restraints of our room. Totally ramped up from the clinic day, I quickly freshened up and we headed out the door to grab some fresh mountain air and good food.

We didn't need to drive far before we spotted a quaint, log-style restaurant just down the road from our hotel. We had just parked the car and hopped out when once again we found ourselves on the receiving end of Bend's hospitality. There was a large group of people conversing and laughing in the parking lot when we pulled in who turned and waved a friendly hello as we headed toward the restaurant. Kristin looked at me with complete surprise as she remarked, "That is totally weird, mom—do you know them from somewhere?" Dumbfounded, I just shook my head, and thinking of Pennsylvania culture, said, "Just keep moving, hun; this can't be good." But as we proceeded to briskly walk away, someone from this curious but overly-friendly group shouted out, "So, where you from? Do you live in Oregon?"

Deciding that they must be fairly harmless, we changed direction and strolled over to join them. After a surprisingly interesting conversation we turned to head back to the restaurant, feeling like we had just made some new friends, again.

Dinner was another delightful experience in this restaurant. The décor was warm and rustic, and our table was situated beside an open-air view of the beautiful mountainside stream. The crystal-clear, sparkling water flowed like a bubbling brook down the mountainside and along the back end of the restaurant. The soothing sounds of this natural wonder were so subliminal, peaceful, and relaxing. I found myself thinking, *I could really live here*, and the clean, invigorating, mountain air was so therapeutic to the soul.

After another unique dining experience, we once again found ourselves exhausted and ready to hit the hay. As we headed back to our hotel, we decided to take a quick detour to a nearby Dairy Queen. Armed with our late-night snack, we headed back to the hotel to wind down our evening with more mom-daughter time and a good movie.

We both must have fallen asleep before the movie ended, because I awoke early the next morning to nothing but static on the TV and the sounds of my daughter snoring.

As I got ready for Saturday morning's "fellowship and farewell" at the ranch, I felt an overwhelming sadness, knowing I'd be leaving this beautiful, mountainous countryside and the united group of new friends I had made at Crystal Peaks, all with similar ministries in their minds and in their hearts. We had all traveled here from different states and different cultures but stood on common ground with one thing—to return home armed with the necessary tools to create our very own similar ministries. Determined to be fully equipped to start up my own similar ministry, I excitedly got dressed, ready to bolt out the door for our last day of encouragement and inspiration. I didn't want to miss a single minute of it.

Chapter 18

Homeward Bound

Psalm 25:4-5

"Show me the right path, O Lord; point out the road for me to follow. Lead me by your truth and teach me, for you are the God who saves me. All day long I put my hope in you" (New Living Translation).

Our final day at Crystal Peaks began with the usual early-morning gatherings around a huge continental-style breakfast, complete with panoramic views of the Cascades. After all the small talk and formalities were done, and contact info was traded amongst our new ranch friends, we proceeded to the Red Rock Meeting Hall for our last fellowship together as a group.

It was a very low-key morning, which focused mainly on fellowship, commission, and prayer. After morning worship with Troy, we gathered with our prayer partners, meeting them face-to-face for the first time. During the entire four days of the info clinic we had never met our prayer partner, until now. When we first arrived at the ranch, on day one, everyone received a card from our assigned prayer partner. This card contained Bible scriptures and many words of encouragement. We knew someone was praying for us, watching us, and getting to know us from afar, but their identity was kept hidden from us until this moment. After introductions, we strolled to a quiet area where we could talk. We swapped personal stories and testimonials before devoting the remainder of our time to encouragement and prayer. We talked about my goals and hopes for the ministry, then prayed for wisdom and guidance with the planning and launching phases of the non-profit. As I hugged my special prayer partner good-bye, she handed me a personalized card, and inside the card was this special verse: 2 Corinthians 1:3-4 (NIV), "Praise be to the God and Father of our Lord Jesus Christ, the Father of compassion and the God of all comfort, who comforts us in all our troubles, so that we can comfort those in any trouble with the comfort we ourselves receive from God."

With eyes that were misted over with happy tears, I headed back to the meeting hall, where Troy concluded the info clinic and opened up the room for discussion and questions.

As I sat in this cozy and rustic meeting room, hastily taking notes, I glanced around at all of my newfound friends and wondered how many of us would leave here and be successful at starting our non-profit ministries. I glanced out the window and was astonished to see a snow squall that had appeared out of the blue. Just minutes before, it was sunny and warm. I remembered what Troy had mentioned to us on Friday, that the weather in Oregon was so unpredictable. It could start out as a warm, sunny day, with temps in the 80s, then within minutes could drop into the 50s with snow, rain, or a severe wind storm that kicks up the infamous dust devils. This reminded me of how life can sometimes be, with all of its ups and downs, twists and turns. Just when things are seemingly going well, a tsunami of events rushes in and with tidal-wave force, upheaves and destroys everything in its path. I have learned, however, that if I am patient and trust God and His timing, He can turn the worst of situations into a miracle.

The weather extremes in Oregon was one of the things I loved most—waking up to 30-40 degrees of fresh, brisk mountain air, then feeling the warmth on my face and shedding my jacket to enjoy the sun's rays just a few hours later.

In closing, Troy presented us with a nice surprise when he baptized one of their staff members in the horses' watering trough. It had stopped snowing and was raining rather heavily when we all headed outside to witness this unusual "practice" at Crystal Peaks. I later learned that this unique demonstration has become a regular ritual of some of the similar ministries at Crystal Peaks. Of course, there is the required duty of cleaning the trough before the actual submergence of the newly-reborn believer. It has become a deep tradition that is performed purely with the serious undertone of announcing to those present the remarkable salvation Jesus offers to all who choose Him. This is just another prime example of how loving and down-to-earth Kim and Troy Meeder actually are.

At Crystal Peaks Youth Ranch, with the
Sister Cascade Mt. Range in the background.

The last few hours spent at Crystal Peaks were a mixture of casual discussions and tearful good-byes. My departure from the ranch was bittersweet as I walked down the driveway, jumped onto the back of the old Ford pick-up one last time, and waved good-bye to my friends as we drove down the road and out of sight.

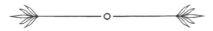

Before Kristin and I had to be at the airport for our return flight, we decided to head downtown to Bend one last time and grab a late lunch. We ended up at a very unique yet upscale restaurant that had available dining on two levels. After very little wait time, a friendly host led us up the stairs and to a cozy little space situated by numerous large picture windows. This allowed for the most spectacular panoramic view of all the hustle and bustle below us on main street in Bend.

Once again, we were completely overwhelmed by the genuine display of friendliness and thoughtfulness from the locals. Not only was our waiter punctual and courteous, but personal as well. He never appeared rushed when taking our order or seeing to our requests, but took time to ask us personal things like where we were from and what our plans were while visiting Bend. He truly seemed interested in us as people, and not merely as another paying customer.

Following our waiter's recommendation, we ordered three unique and tantalizing appetizers to share. Then we settled back in our chairs to reminisce over the last few days and enjoy this rare moment of being together with no pressing agenda to rush off to.

While we sat waiting for our check, the biggest surprise happened when our gracious waiter returned to say, "Your meals have been paid for, and this person wants to remain anonymous." Well, needless to say, I was totally blown away by this random act of kindness; but what a perfect way to complete our wonderful trip to Oregon.

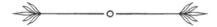

As Kristin and I walked across the airport parking lot toward our waiting plane, I glanced back at the Cascade mountains looming in the distance. I took a deep, cleansing breath, letting all the fresh mountain air fill my lungs, and thought to myself, *This is where it all began, where my dream, my goals, my purpose—His purpose—are taking flight.* This plane that would be flying us back home would be transporting me from this beautiful place of refuge, encouragement, and learning at Crystal Peaks to the beginning of my ministry and Haven of Hope: "Where a rescue horse can connect with troubled youth and together find acceptance, healing, and restored hope."

As I turned and boarded the plane, I felt like we were stepping into a huge time-warp machine, and that my life as I once knew it was over and a new life—complete with my childhood dreams and purpose—was about to begin.

Epilogue

Hope Heals is a testament of how God can restore hope and offer healing to the brokenhearted by using the unique and strong connections formed between a broken and wounded rescue horse and that of a hurting child. Horses that have been subjected to abuse, neglect, or other forms of trauma can often identify with people who have experienced similar backgrounds.

Hope, both in the literal and metaphoric sense, is described within the pages of this book.

Our buckskin horse named Hope was the first rescue horse that remained at Hope's Haven and has become an integral part of the mentorship program. She is our namesake and freely offers love, acceptance, and hope to all who have the opportunity to meet her.

Hope, in the metaphoric sense, offers light in a darkened world and strength and encouragement to those struggling to survive; it helps people to make sense of a tragedy or to deal with traumatic issues that have left them feeling desperate and hopeless. This kind of hope can only be found and is freely given by our awesome and Almighty God.

The previous stories are very personal and dear to my heart. They chronicle the events surrounding the individual horses rescued between 2016-2017 and the lives they touched while in our care or within the mentorship program at Hope's Haven.

Author's Notes

This book was completed in 2021, during the international COVID-19 pandemic. This greatly impacted many businesses and non-profits, with many unable to continue due to lack of finances and having to permanently close their doors. God is good, and faithful, and it has always been my belief that what God has helped me to build, He will provide for and sustain. Thankfully, because of our extremely loyal volunteers and supportive donors, we were able to keep our doors open during this extremely challenging time.

The following is a timeline of major events from the initial incorporation of Hope's Haven Rescue and Youth Camp up to 2020:

Timeline of Hope's Haven from May 2017-December 2020:

May 2017: Diane traveled to Bend, Oregon to attend Kim and Troy Meeder's info clinic. It was there that she learned how to make her vision a reality.

March 2018: Hope's Haven Rescue and Youth Camp was born and officially became a 501(c)(3) non-profit. This was our first season in operation as a ministry within our mentorship program.

June 9, 2018: Our first-ever fundraiser event, a chicken BBQ, held at Bainbridge's Conoy Park West. Not a huge success.

October 2018: Hope's Haven's first fall fundraiser event, Hope's Hoedown

December 2018: Our first Christmas party/open house for the mentorship kids, families, and the public.

May 25, 2019: Our first spring kick-off event. Not a huge success. Note to self: never plan an event over a holiday weekend such as Memorial Day.

October 19, 2019: Our 2nd annual Hope's Hoedown. This event is quickly becoming a huge favorite.

November 2019: We were so excited and grateful to have the honor of partnering with LCBC (Lives Changed By Christ, one of Lancaster County's largest non-denominational churches) within their annual Be Rich initiative. This made a huge impact on the future of Hope's Haven and our ministry.

December 15, 2019: Our 2nd annual Christmas party for the mentorship kids and families.

March 2020: a deadly virus, coronavirus (COVID-19), struck and became a global pandemic. By the end of the month the governor had ordered everyone to "shelter in place." This forced all schools and businesses to close. Leaving the house was only allowed if absolutely necessary, such as to travel to a place of employment, the grocery store, the drug store, or the doctor. Wearing a face mask when out in public became mandatory. This continued until June 2020 and negatively affected businesses worldwide, forcing many to close their doors permanently. Hope's Haven was also affected in that we had to cancel all of our annual fundraisers, which hurt us terribly.

June 2020: We officially opened our doors for our mentorship program despite the COVID-19 pandemic. New rules were put in place to safeguard volunteers, mentor kids, families, and the community. The entire barn got wiped down and sanitized twice a day, and masks were to be worn at all times when in the barn or when less than six feet apart from another person.

August 22, 2020: Hope's Haven's first benefit yard sale. Because of the COVID-19 pandemic we were forced to cancel most of our annual fundraiser events. The yard sale was the only event we were able to hold during the summer. It was a huge success!

October 24, 2020: Hope's Haven's 3rd annual Hope's Hoedown fundraiser event. Three different activities we incorporated this year were: a kids' obstacle course; a David & Goliath challenge; and a spectacular hayride, taken to the rescue farm where our current rescue horses are housed. Another huge success!

November 7, 2020: The close of our mentorship season for this year.

December 18, 2020: Hope's Haven's 3rd annual Christmas party for mentor kids, families, and volunteers. Due to the COVID-19 pandemic we had to be creative and do things differently this year. So, we did a walk-through event. We began with a live nativity scene outside the rear entrance, then had a "photo op" station where the kids could have their picture taken with their favorite horse, wearing a Santa hat. Their next stop was at the front end of the barn, where the kids could meet Santa and his elf helper to receive their gifts and personalized stockings. Their last stop as they headed out the door was at the hot food table, where their dinner and hot drinks were packed up in to-go containers along with baggies of homemade Christmas cookies.

Everyone absolutely loved this event, especially the kids. What a way to end 2020.

About the Author

Diane grew up on a 110-acre dairy farm in Lancaster County, Pennsylvania. The second-to-youngest of eight children, she rarely received any new or fancy items, as most were hand-me downs passed on from older siblings. From apparel to bicycles, by the time these items reached her hands they were not always in the best of condition.

However, as she fondly recalls, "I learned to appreciate this later in life, as it taught me what was really important—that real value was not found in material things.

"There were always plenty of animals around for a young girl to spend her time with, but horses have always held a very special place in my heart, then and now. For as long as I can remember, I have always felt a strong desire to help hurting kids and horses. What started as a childhood dream later became a vision, and then a calling, or what I felt was God's purpose for my life."

Being a member of a large family and living on a working dairy farm taught her so much about life. Not only did she develop an excellent work ethic, but she also learned the meaning of teamwork as she worked alongside her brothers and sisters every day. But probably the most important thing she learned at a very young age was to never give up on your goals and dreams. If you want something badly enough and are willing to work hard to obtain it, and if you truly believe it's what God wants for your life, He can carry you through it, and you can achieve it.

At age twenty-three Diane married her first husband and by age twenty-six had her beautiful daughter, Kristin. Unfortunately, after almost ten years of lies, manipulation, unfaithfulness, and emotional turmoil, the marriage dissolved, and at the age of thirty-two she suddenly found herself all alone. The impact of this separation of family was felt far beyond what could have ever been imagined—she was suddenly thrown into a life as a single mother to a very confused and devastated five-year-old girl.

After the divorce, feeling totally betrayed and destroyed—and having lost so much of herself and her life in those ten years—she was determined to resurrect her goals, desires, and dreams, and to finally accomplish each and every one of them.

With head held high, and with a powerful determination, she forged onward to accomplish not only her goals but God's all-revealing purpose for her life. By age forty, she had put herself through school and had obtained her associates in nursing degree, working in various fields of nursing which included ten years in hospital med-surg and rehab nursing; five years as a school nurse, caring for both elementary and middle school aged kids; three years as a nursing supervisor at two different nursing facilities; as well as assisting in the twenty-four-hour in-home care of her aging mother and father.

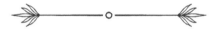

In September of 2013, another chapter began in Diane's life. At the mature age of forty-eight, and after spending more than sixteen years learning, growing, and becoming a much stronger person, God placed the perfect man into her life. He knew what she needed, even if she didn't. The complete irony of how they met could only have been as a result of the all-mighty Creator Himself.

Having grown up on a working farm himself, Steve and Diane had lived in the same neighborhood and attended the same schools their entire lives, yet had never physically met until that autumn day in 2013.

Interestingly enough, as Diane later learned, Steve had often helped her father with field work as a teenager, as well as working for the neighbor across the street for many years. All of these "near misses," when their paths had almost—but never—crossed, had to have been God's ultimate plan for their lives. Because they had never met face to face until that one day in September, when they acciden-tally happened upon each other outside a cornfield. It was here, on the property where Diane was currently living, that their two lives intersected for the first time, and on April 8, 2016, they began their journey together as husband and wife.

During the initial fifteen years of her nursing career, Diane often felt like there was something greater God had in store for her. "I never could shake the overwhelming feeling that my God-given purpose was not yet fulfilled." She continued to revisit the idea of helping at-risk horses and hurting kids. So, in May of 2017, she made her dream and vision a reality when she registered for one of Crystal Peaks' info clinics. It was there that she learned everything she needed to start up a similar ministry like that of Crystal Peaks, and that was where her real story of ministry began.

Me and Steve at Kristin's wedding-Aug. 21, 2021

In Loving Memory
(October 2006–April 2021):

During the editing phase of this book, we were saddened by the loss of our dog, Buddy. For fifteen years he served not only as a best friend but also a faithful companion and travel buddy. He loved the daily trips to Hope's Haven to visit the horses and other animals. Over the years he was fondly thought of as our canine mascot. You will surely be missed, Buddy. Gone, but never forgotten.